MISSION ACCOMPLISHED!

Praise for the book

The author traces the symbiotic relationship between defence and industry and how time-tested military principles can be applied in business, management and day-to-day life.
—**Lt Gen. K.T. Parnaik**, PVSM, UYSM, YSM, former Northern Army Commander

The spirit and art of soldiering and the underlying principles of war to achieve the mission and their implications in management sciences have been encapsulated lucidly. This is a primer for the uninitiated and a source of intro spection for the professionals.
—**Gautam Sen**, Professor Emeritus—Management Institute of Learning & Excellence, Pune

MISSION ACCOMPLISHED!

APPLYING MILITARY PRINCIPLES TO REAL LIFE

VIRENDER KAPOOR

RUPA

Published by
Rupa Publications India Pvt. Ltd 2021
7/16, Ansari Road, Daryaganj
New Delhi 110002

Sales centres:
Allahabad Bengaluru Chennai
Hyderabad Jaipur Kathmandu
Kolkata Mumbai

Copyright © Virender Kapoor 2021

All rights reserved.
No part of this publication may be reproduced, transmitted,
or stored in a retrieval system, in any form or by any means,
electronic, mechanical, photocopying, recording or otherwise,
without the prior permission of the publisher.

The views and opinions expressed in this book are
the author's own and the facts are as reported by him
which have been verified to the extent possible,
and the publishers are not in any way liable for the same.

ISBN: 978-93-90547-94-4

First impression 2021

10 9 8 7 6 5 4 3 2 1

The moral right of the author has been asserted.

Printed at Thomson Press India Ltd, Faridabad

This book is sold subject to the condition that it shall not,
by way of trade or otherwise, be lent, resold, hired out, or otherwise
circulated, without the publisher's prior consent, in any form of
binding or cover other than that in which it is published.

Contents

Preface *vii*

1. Improvization: Being Resourceful — 1
2. Morale and Esprit de Corps: The Man Behind the Gun — 17
3. Blitzkrieg: Lightning Warfare — 44
4. Force Multipliers: The Game Changers — 63
5. Economy of Effort and Concentration of Force — 90
6. Propaganda: Creating Virtual Reality — 105
7. Surprise and Deception: Hit When He Least Expects It — 129
8. Credible Deterrence: How to Avoid a Conflict — 156
9. Mobilization: Building and Maintaining Resources — 178
10. Teeth-to-Tail Ratio: Maximum Bang for the Buck — 215
11. Principle of 'One Leg on the Ground': Safety First — 243
12. Camouflage and Concealment: Merge with the Background — 248
13. Selection and Maintenance of Aim: Vision and Mission — 254
14. Tactical Retreat: How Far Is Too Far? — 260

Bibliography — 265

Preface

The Art of War by Sun Tzu, written around 500 BCE, is not only seen as a precursor to modern military doctrines and guide for modern military leaders, but has also been cleverly adapted by business and political leadership throughout the world. Even after 25 centuries, it remains a valuable piece of literature for the conduct of war and applied politics. Tzu talks of the strategy and broad principles that form the basis of conducting warfare or handling the affairs of a nation state at the political level. Though horses and spears have been replaced by tanks, aircraft and powerful weapons, including nuclear armaments, Tzu's teachings still remain relevant because he deals with the fundamentals of warfare, including how it's influenced by human behaviour, politics and the compulsions of a nation state. International relations have also gone through a sea change, yet these basic foundation stones can be easily adapted even in today's complex global environment by a head of the state, a general, a diplomat, a business honcho, a manager or a politician operating at a strategic or tactical level.

These eternal truths were enumerated by Tzu when there was no management science, and at a time when very little technological or scientific innovations had happened. These, therefore, are the very basic ideas on military and political philosophy, which are applicable across ages.

While Tzu looks at fundamentals, this book examines the principles that define military methods to accomplish an operational task in a military campaign.

These principles define a military action, process or methodology to accomplish a particular task, a strategic intent or used effectively in a particular military scenario. These have gradually evolved over centuries of warfare but have been adapted as well as modified over time. Such modifications happened due to the modernization of weapon systems and technology, and changing international power equations, geopolitics and warfare scenarios. These are fully developed ideas and methods that can be applied to any complex civilian scenario, business or otherwise. They can also be seen as time-tested operational principles, which we have a lot to learn from.

Several management principles, therefore, have either been evolved or are a derivative of such practices, and are followed by armed forces across the world. Areas like leadership, motivation, human resource management, business strategy, business ethics, inventory management, organizational behaviour, organizational structure, project management, team work and stress management have benefitted the most from military practices. These methods were used successfully under the most trying circumstances and possibly learnt at a heavy price during military operations in which millions perished. That is the reason why they have been adopted wholeheartedly by the management sciences and are being used effectively as models of excellence.

The area of applied technology as well as pure sciences have also highly benefitted from warfare techniques over the centuries. This happened because every country was investing a substantial amount of their annual budgets in creating military edge over their adversaries. These technological feats, when added to military management practices, had a force multiplication effect on military operations.

Eventually, every participating nation state profited from this, as they could recycle the same cutting edge technology for civilian use, popularly known as dual-use technology. This could be used for both peaceful commercial applications as well as military ones, and positively influence a country's economy as it would boost nuclear power generation, missile and space missions, telecommunications, applied electronics, the chemical industry, automobiles, and all branches of engineering and medical science.

The idea behind writing this book was to explore each one of these strategic as well as tactical operational processes, principles and methods, and examining 'core values' that can be applied across a broad spectrum of situations in our daily lives as well as businesses. The impact and influence of technology and the geopolitical transition of these principles have been adequately added as part of the context. I have studied these principles over a period of time and I am convinced that this work can also become a very meaningful manual for business strategy and tactics.

Each chapter first explains a basic concept and then analyses them from the perspective of actual military operations from the last century, including the two great World Wars. This illustrates the expanse of their application, despite the widely divergent situations. Each chapter thereafter, briefly examines the application of that sole principle in our daily life as well as business, work or wherever applicable.

This book is an amalgamation of various disciplines like contemporary history, science and technology, management sciences, engineering, psychology, information technology (IT), telematics, leadership, motivation, human resource management, management economics, military history, strategy and tactics, weaponry, geography, geopolitics, international relations, diplomacy and political science.

I have hands-on experience of using these principles and some of the systems, and have witnessed them being used at all levels of the military hierarchy. I was also fortunate to be a part of the research and development (R&D) of some of these fascinating systems.

I am certain that this will be an interesting and a valuable read for a large number of people from different age groups, and professional and academic backgrounds.

1

Improvization: Being Resourceful

'Prepare for the unknown by studying how others in the past have coped with the unforeseeable and the unpredictable.'
—General George S. Patton

What is Improvization?

Improvization is doing something without advance planning. It can be an impromptu speech or joining two single beds to make a double bed if the occasion so demands.

Improvization is possible in almost all facets of our personal and professional life. It is intended to solve an unexpected problem at hand, which needs to be considered as priority and fixed immediately. It is a stopgap arrangement. For instance, if someone meets with an accident and breaks a bone at a place where no medical help is available, one could tie up the injured part of the body with wooden splinters to immobilize the limb till the patient is taken to a hospital where a proper plaster can be cast after medical examination. This temporary arrangement is sufficient to prevent further damage and provide adequate support to the injured person as well as help ease out the pain.

Military Improvizations

Armed forces were probably the first ones to adopt Improvization as a part of their ethos. At different levels, every military operation throws up several unexpected situations and challenges. However, despite impeccable planning by the military commander, there are several parameters that are neither in his control nor can they ever be predicted.

The conduct of military operations is subject to the same imperfections as any other field, but has an additional burden of saving or destroying several human lives. In war, blunders are made from the lowest to the highest levels. Therefore, in this context, improvization can become a saviour of sorts, whether for a short-term issue or longer one.

The Second World War was possibly the longest and the bloodiest war of the last century where around 40 countries got into a conflict. Many military lessons were learnt at a heavy cost. Such was the speed, expanse and unpredictability of military operations that field commanders were often left with no choice but to resort to improvization.

Tactical Improvization

In the Second World War, the German military potential declined continually, and towards the end, their equipment and soldiers were almost insignificant in comparison to the Russians. Therefore, improvizations in combat were rampant. At the end, the entire conduct of war on the eastern front was one great improvization. It was also used across the war zone for tactical, technical and even logistical management.

Initially, German tanks organized as Panzer divisions created havoc by unleashing a lightning warfare popularly known as 'blitzkrieg'. Every week, they advanced hundreds of miles into Russian territory until winter arrived and unexpected rain and snow bogged them down. By the end of December 1941, the sixth Panzer division, which had more than 200 tanks and artillery support, was slowed by the slush and mud. They had to withdraw and lost every tank and gun, and many soldiers died because of the cold and hunger. In January 1942, once they had reassembled, all that remained was around 60 men and only three guns.

As a desperate measure, all non-combatants, road-building battalions and supply units from the rear areas were called to make ad hoc alert units. Men and officers from the same unit were clubbed together to maintain a sense of camaraderie. Therefore, such units, despite their varied strengths, possessed a sense of uniformity within. As food supplies were minimal and soldiers were dying of cold and hunger, orders were passed for people to wrap themselves with paper—even toilet paper— to save them from the biting cold.

Numerous examples can be quoted when improvization was adopted for logistics and supply. During summers, when German armoured columns advanced across the Russian plains, they looked down upon horses pulling heavy peasant wagons. They were dismissed by Germans as 'a hundred years behind time'. But as winter set in, both armies had to bank on horses to move their essential equipment, transporting the wounded and essential food supplies as no other mechanical transport could move in the thick mud. Some German Panzer divisions employed more than 2,000 horses. Though this was initially a case of adhocism; gradually responding to this need, regular mule transport or animal transport battalions were created in almost all the armies to operate in mountains and snow-bound areas.

The corduroy road was again a contraption built to survive bad weather. It is a typical log road made by placing thin wooden logs perpendicular to the direction of the road in swampy areas. The war could not have continued in swampy regions of Russia had these roads not been built. This was the most important improvization for the Eastern Theatre of war. In the middle of 1941, during the offensive on Leningrad, an entire Panzer corps with more than 500 tanks and integral artillery got stuck for many days in swampy forests. Corduroy roads were quickly built and the tanks started rolling out to mount an offensive.

For foot soldiers, crossing mine fields is a major problem. Usually, safe lanes are created by engineer detachments in advance. During the first few years of the Second World War, the Germans were advancing rapidly on all fronts and therefore, this procedure became a major reason for the delay in their scheme of things. German infantry commanders came up with innovative improvizational options to overcome this. Since the enemy was also laying mines in a hurry, most mines left some telltale marks, which were visible to the naked eye. It was decided to quickly train infantry soldiers to locate these mines by visual inspection. In many places, dry grass and a little depression or difference in the colour of the soil facilitated the spotting. Once spotted, a small marker was placed next to individual mines, creating a safe way for the troops to avoid being blown up while crossing. For better results, soldiers were trained in captured enemy mine fields.

Improvising Weapons

Some bizarre weapons have been created by improvization. When the German army was attacking Russia, the Red Army was thinking of innovative methods of killing the Nazis. One such contraption was created by mounting the telescope of a rifle on a giant 14.5-mm anti-tank rifle to kill Germans hiding in bunkers. It fired a huge explosive shell (meant to destroy a tank) into a bunker through its viewing slits, which blew the bunker inside out. This technique was improvised to create 'pillboxes'—very strong bunkers with outer shells that cannot be destroyed easily.

During a withdrawal operation, the withdrawing army suffers heavy causalities because the enemy gets an opportunity to inflict the maximum damage on the troops. During the Gallipoli campaign during the First World War, the Allied forces decided to withdraw from a not-so-lucrative holding position. They knew that the enemy would come down heavily on them as thousands of their soldiers moved back.

Two of their soldiers built a contraption using old ration tins, allowing water to drip from one to another to trigger a rifle to fire a gun all by itself. Several such guns were positioned and they fired one by one as troops withdrew. Instead of experiencing large casualties, the Allied forces managed to escape with only a few dead.

Improvised military vehicles for combat are sometimes created by modifying civilian vehicles. They are strengthened by adding armour plating and are armed by mounting weapon systems onto them. These are not only used by guerrilla forces but also by regular armies. Earlier versions were called armoured cars or armoured personnel carriers (APCs). During the Second World War, Russians created an ad hoc or improvised Armoured Fighting Vehicle (AFV) by mounting a gun on an STZ-5 agriculture tractor. This was fabricated to create fear among the enemy. During the Second World War, the British created 'gun trucks' by using commercial Bedford trucks and mounting anti-tank guns and machine guns. They also created mobile pillboxes by mounting concrete fighting compartments on commercial trucks. During the Iraq war, American logistics convoys came under heavy attack, which forced them to create a gun truck, based on a M939 5-ton truck, to prevent casualties.

Training and Manpower Development: An Improvizational Attitude

In the armed forces, talent acquisition and training are very specialized tasks. For the officers' selection, a Services Selection Board (SSB) conducts a rigorous and elaborate interview process spread over several days. The instinct of improvization is also an important parameter, basis which the selection is done. Group tasks are conducted by a Group Task Officer (GTO) where a candidate is given a team and a few props, like planks, ropes, wires, empty barrels and tyres, etc. The candidate needs to apply his ingenuity to use all these props carefully and intelligently to perform the given task. This forms a major part of the GTO's assessment process, and improvization is at the centre of it.

During the training of officers and cadets, improvization may not be taught as a subject, but it is always built into training exercises and discussions wherever applicable. During commando training, one learns to cook food without utensils, using banana leaves and mud as substitutes. During frequent operational moves, one manages to live with very little, trying to use whatever is available. In a way, this becomes part of a soldier's attitude for life.

I remember going for training exercises in the winters at the Indian Military Academy. Each of us was to carry our rations, blankets and clothing in our backpacks and we were carrying just the essentials. December and January are very cold on the mountaintops. It used to be a nightmare at night, as a couple of blankets and a sheet to lie on would not be sufficient for a person to stay warm. Therefore, four of us would huddle together with a few sheets and blankets on the ground and six blankets and two sheets over us, forming four layers on top. Boots were used as pillows. We always looked for a depression in the ground to put up this 'warm hole' to save us from the chilly winds. Every piece of equipment was used to cover ourselves.

Spies and Agents: Improvization in Espionage

A military commander has men, equipment, weapons and resources in a war. As a contrast, a spy largely operates alone. He or she has very little resources and operates in an alien, often unchartered and hostile geographical location. To make it worse, he has to mostly operate undercover. Therefore, for a spy, presence of mind and improvization are essential skills. Even if he has a plan, there is no certainty or backup and he cannot take chances. His ingenuity and spur-of-the-moment decisions, based on how things unfold, become life-saving skills.

If one has to illustrate this, then James Bond comes first to mind. He uses almost anything that he finds to defend himself and kill his opponent. In one scene, he uses a cigarette lighter to light up the nozzle of a cologne, transforming it into a small flamethrower to kill a snake. In yet another scene, he throws alcohol on an opponent posing as a waiter and carrying sizzling barbeque skewers, which causes a major fire and kills his opponent. Similarly, during the Cold War, Central Intelligence Agency (CIA) and Committee for State Security (KGB) spies had to come up with considerable spontaneity and improvization to get out of life-threatening situations.

Non-State Actors: Terrorists, Guerillas and Insurgents

Nation states have fully equipped their armed forces with weapons and logistical support. In contrast, non-state actors who have emerged on the scene during the last 50 to 60 years have to mostly improvise upon their arsenal. They also aim to derive 'maximum bang for the buck', literally, and hence come up with innovative and effective ways of using whatever they can lay their hands on to balance the inherent asymmetry.

Improvised Explosive Devices (IEDs) are homemade bombs assembled and used in a non-conventional way. They could be made partly by using military explosives, unexploded bombs and a timer detonator. The term originated during the Irish Home Rule movement in the 1970s. The Irish Republic Army used bombs made of fertilizers, which were used as booby traps against the British. Over a period of time, radically different IEDs were manufactured by different groups. In the Iraq War, IEDs were responsible for almost 63 per cent casualities among the US-led coalition forces.

While the warheads used in IEDs included explosives, chemicals, incendiaries and even biological equipment, the delivery mechanisms ranged from cars, boats, cycles, animals, two wheelers, rockets to even human bombs. Usually, cell phones, radio signals or wires were used as triggers.

During the Vietnam War, soldiers from the National Liberation Front used out-of-the-box ideas to use grenades. They pulled out the pin of a grenade with the clip intact, and put it into a tin. The grenade was then attached to a string acting as a trip wire. Once there was pressure on the string, the grenade fell out, releasing the clip to detonate the grenade.

They also used the 'rubber band' grenade, which was nothing but a grenade with the safety pin removed and the clip held by a rubber band. Such grenades were placed in huts, which were burnt regularly by the Americans. The moment a hut caught fire, the rubber bands melted, releasing the safety lever, blowing up the hut, the bamboo and metal fragments and killing the American soldiers. Such rubber band bombs were also put in enemy vehicle petrol tanks. Once the rubber band corroded due to the chemical action of fuel, the grenade exploded. Jar grenades were also used, in which a primed grenade was put into a glass jar. As the jar hit a wall or the ground, it shattered and the grenade exploded. This was used in helicopter warfare extensively.

The most primitive timing device was a tin half filled with chickpeas and then topped with water. The mouth of the tin was tightly covered by a lid, which was then connected to a detonator mechanism. After a few hours, the chickpeas fermented, bloated and pushed the lid upwards, making a contact with the trigger mechanism and exploding the attached bomb.

Molotov cocktails, or homemade petrol bombs, are used in urban guerrilla warfare. These bombs are made by using a breakable glass bottle filled with a mixture of petrol and diesel, and a cloth wick. It explodes on impact, causing a fireball and plenty of damage.

Medical Improvization

Improvization was not only used for warfare, spying and killing people, but often to save lives during wars, as in such situations, doctors are always short of the right medicines and equipment.

During the Second World War, a number of Australian prisoners of war were put up in camps and employed to construct the Thai-Burma Railway track. Since medical equipment was scarce in these camps, the medical personnel had to often resort to improvization. Many medical tools were created out of whatever was available. Bamboo was a major resource and was used to make water and food containers, brooms, needles, latrines and even bed pans for the seriously injured. Cutlery was hammered and sharpened to make surgical instruments, and scrap metal was used to make forceps, curettes and scalpels.

Richard Rowley, an Australian doctor and prisoner of war who later wrote a book called *A Doctor's War*, says, 'We made surgical instruments out of scrap stolen from railway stores. All the doctors in the camp became skilled at the art of improvization. They used bamboos as stethoscopes and instead used the tubing of stethoscopes for drips and blood transfusion. They even made artificial limbs, pneumonia jackets, splints, stretchers and scalpels as well as stitching needles from Bamboo.'

In *Improvised Medicine*, the author Kenneth Iserson says that at the heart of medicine in the wilderness is improvization, which is a creative amalgam of formal medical science and common sense. Such skills are required for doctors who are a part of rescue teams or accompanying adventurous expeditions.

A lot of work has been done in this area, which includes wound management, handling trauma, dressings and bandages, orthopedic injuries, blister management and even the improvised transportation of patients.

Improvization: Entertainment, Art and Craft

One may be surprised to know the level of improvization that is used by people who are in the entertainment industry.

Actors are great improvisers on stage. Having rehearsed for a play repeatedly does not guarantee a flawless performance. One may forget a dialogue, a certain prop may not work or a wardrobe malfunction may occur. A good actor quickly improvises and handles the situation flawlessly. After a remarkable play performed by veteran Bollywood actors Naseeruddin Shah and his wife Ratna Pathak Shah, we sat in the audience as both of them came on the stage and spoke to us. One lady from the audience got up and asked, 'How do you manage to give such a flawless performance?'

He responded with a big grin on his face, 'Do you know that in today's performance we made close to fifty mistakes! But none of you could spot them because we managed to handle each such situation.' This is nothing but improvising on the spot!

Standup comedy requires a great sense of timing and improvization. The actor often interacts with the audience and responds to questions, remarks and suggestions, which are instantaneous. Spontaneous actors adapt themselves according to their co-actors, the situation and the director.

Even directors improvise. Though today everything is scripted and rehearsed, directors need to know how to turn a negative situation into a positive one instantly. The director of *Paranormal Activity*, Oren Peli, says that the actors he casted were relatively new, with little experience. He had explained to them their characters, but they were not really memorizing their lines and it was always spontaneous. This improvizational technique made the film very authentic and convincing.

Street plays are often quickly put together with minimum props. The audience could be perched up on trees or standing on the road in a big circle. These plays require a great amount of ingenuity, thinking on one's feet and a great mind for improvization.

Some writers are also very spontaneous and move with the flow. If they get a new idea, they quickly integrate it into the narrative. Such writing is racy and throws many curveballs at the reader. I feel that as an author grows, she becomes more creative due to spontaneity and improvization.

Improvizational theatre is a new form of performing arts where the content and script are created instantaneously. It is an extension of experimental theatre where the actors may engage with the audience in different ways. The act often progresses according to the audience's response.

Flash Mob

A flash mob is large group of people who perform an unusual or seemingly random act, usually organized through social media, and then disperse just as suddenly as they had appeared. These could be organized in response to an event or to gather the attention of people to generate a favourable public opinion for a purpose. These are an ad hoc group of people who can make a considerable impact and achieve the desired result without much investment, planning or preparation. In that sense, flash mobs are improvised events.

Improvization in Engineering

The most astonishing example of engineering improvization was undertaken aboard the Apollo 13, the seventh manned mission in the American Space Program. After only 54 hours in space, the mission had been aborted after the explosion of an oxygen tank, which had crippled the service module of the space ship that supported the command module. Despite a shortage of water, limited power and difficulty in removing carbon dioxide from the manned modules, the crew had to improvise a critical component—a carbon dioxide scrubber cartridge—which had been manufactured differently for the command module and the lunar module. Using whatever was available at hand, astronaut J.L. Swigert rigged things in such a way that a square carbon dioxide scrubber cartridge was fitted into the lunar module, which could only fit a round—a literal instance of the old adage, 'Trying to fit a square peg into a round hole.'

Improvization and out-of-the-box thinking have been displayed by many people in the manufacturing industry as well. A soap-manufacturing company was finding it difficult to automate the wrapping of soaps and putting them into cartons using a conveyer belt. At times, the soap cake was missed and the wrapping machine wrapped the paper without a soap. The plant manager was struggling to find a solution and asked for suggestions. The R&D team suggested installing some laser-based sensors, while few suggested an even more expensive X-ray machine to detect such errors. However, one smart supervisor suggested that they instal a simple table fan at the end of the conveyer belt to blow away the empty wrappers, preventing them from entering the carton.

Cannibalization is an important way to maintain equipment. Engineers in large organizations resort to removing serviceable parts from damaged equipment, which they use for repairing similar kind of machinery. This becomes very important in the military context because a large number of guns, vehicles and aircraft get damaged during operations. Many critical components can be taken out of these and used to repair the unserviceable equipment right in the field itself. This is a very cost-effective method and can save resources, time as well as money.

I have seen large organizations shifting their offices from one place to the other, leaving behind a number of items they consider worthless. However, there are specialists who are great at making use of the 'best that they can get' out of old things and ensuring zero wastage. A company that is in a cost-cutting mode should look at this option. Cannibalization and improvization may not be identical but they go hand in hand.

During the Second World War, side cars were extensively attached to motorcycles to augment their carrying capacity. By the beginning of the 20th century, motorcycle manufacturers started producing side cars in large numbers. Improvization, innovation, creativity and inventions are closely related. The three-wheeler auto rickshaw is yet another engineering improvization that has helped millions travel within the crowded cities of most developing countries. Karl Benz, a German engine designer, made the first three-wheeled car and got a patent for it way back in 1885.

In the late 1950s, substantial military hardware became available in the civil market. The 750 cc engine Harley Davidson motorcycles were available in abundance, and were used extensively in India, where an improvised chassis and body on two wheels was connected to the powerful Harley front wheel, petrol tank and engine. This was popularly known as the 'Phat-Phat', as it made a lot of noise.

Improvization in the Business Environment

Researchers are always looking for newer skill sets to manage and resolve today's unexpected managerial challenges. One of the areas of concern is making leaders work under pressure and with 'constrained resources'. Working under pressure with few resources triggers creativity, and pushes one towards improvization. This is neither taught in B-schools nor can be imparted through case studies.

Randy Sabourin and Dr R. W. Pratt used The Attention and Interpersonal Style (TAIS) inventory, which uses concentration, working under pressure and other related parameters, to test the abilities of business leaders, using a self-report questionnaire to measure different skills like awareness, flexibility, decision-making styles, etc.[1] It is also used by the US Navy SEALs.

The armed forces have the luxury of conducting large-scale exercises where thousands of troops along with hundreds of vehicles and tanks can take part for periods stretching to a couple of months. These are usually made to feel as real as possible. Military commanders thus get to work under 'real' pressure. On-the-spot decisions have to be made as during the exercise, equipment and vehicles also get damaged, become unserviceable or slow down.

During their training, telecom engineers in the armed forces are provided all the field equipment to actually lay out and configure communication channels and 'go live', providing real communication as desired. Military managers are tasked with indicating the requirement as per an operational

---

[1] Sabourin, R. and Robin W. Pratt. (2013). "Business Improvization Research Paper". Retrieved from http://www.e-roleplay.com/business-improvization-research-paper/

scenario. The equipment that would be available are provided on an equipment table. Each engineer has to come up with a communication layout design in a specific time frame. The equipment that is made available is very limited and only the smartest can possibly reach the desired result. This exercise is popularly called 'Circuit Utilization' or the system design exercise. Once the blueprint is created, the actual equipment is deployed on the ground by the students to physically engineer the network. Telecom engineers undertaking a university programme unfortunately cannot be given such hands-on experience with the equipment and related hardware.

The next 'killer app' will teach business managers and leaders how to improvise their performance and enhance the productivity of their organization. Performing on the spot and under pressure during crises is the next management frontier to maximize return on investment. A lot needs to be done in this area and practical, yet affordable methods and exercises need to be created to improve this skill. A combination of hands-on practices and instant simulation in a classroom could deliver the desired results.

In the Indian context, improvization is nothing but 'jugaad'. Indians are known for being innovative, street smart and resourceful, precisely because they have to often work with limited resources. Every leader at the end of the day must inculcate the jugaad attitude.

2

Morale and Esprit de Corps: The Man Behind the Gun

> *'What counts is not necessarily the size of the dog in the fight, it's the size of the fight in the dog.'*
> —Dwight D. Eisenhower

What Is Morale?

Leading men in battle and making them fight the enemy requires a type of leadership skill and mindset that is different from a leader in any other job. The moral responsibilities of the ground-level troops remain the greatest challenge for military leadership. It also requires building team spirit in the men who fight for their country or for a cause, and are made to willingly lay down their lives. What makes them men of such calibre, value, honour and selflessness? After all, they are the same flesh and blood as anybody else. They belong to the same society and have a similar upbringing as their fellow citizens.

The differentiator is the kind of training that is imparted and a sense of belonging that is built in the uniformed fraternity. This remains in every soldier for the rest of his life. A fighting force can keep fighting as long as it 'feels like' fighting. It is this willingness to fight under all odds that is more important than having weapons and tanks. A fighting force that has this feeling and spirit is supposed to possess high morale.

As World War II army historian General S.L.A. Marshal has said,[2]

> Morale is the thinking of an army. It is the whole complex body of an army's thought. The way it feels about the soil and the people from which it springs. The way it feels about their cause and their politics as compared with other causes and other politics. The way it feels about its friends and allies, as well as its enemies. About its commanders and gold bricks. About food and shelter. Duty and leisure. Payday and sex. Militarism and civilians. Freedom and slavery. Work and want. Weapons and comradeship. Bunk fatigue and drill. Discipline and disorder. Life and death. God and the devil.

The morale of a group concerns the collective group feel as well as the individual feeling of each member of the group. A well-fed, well-equipped army with low morale will stand no chance to win a battle against a highly motivated, charged-up force, which may have inferior provisions.

The 18th century Prussian military theorist Carl Von Clausewitz, a seasoned general, had said,[3]

> Physical casualties are not the only losses incurred by both sides in the course of the engagement: their moral strength is also shaken, broken and ruined. In deciding whether or not to continue the engagement it is not enough to consider the loss of men, horses, and guns; one also has to weigh the loss of order, courage,

---

[2]Marshall, S.L.A. (1947). *Men against Fire: The Problem of Battle Command in Future War.*
[3]Von Clausewitz, C. (1956). *On War* (Vol. 2). Jazzybee Verlag.

confidence, cohesion, and plan. The decision rests chiefly on the state of morale, which, in cases where the victor has lost as much as the vanquished, has always been the single decisive factor.

Different Definitions, yet Similar Interpretations

Morale is such an intangibly tangible entity, that it is not easily definable or measurable. Since the beginning of organized warfare, several definitions have emerged over a period of time as the importance of morale has been realized by military commanders. British Lieutenant Colonel J.G. Shillington gives one such definition: 'Morale can be described as a mental state composed of three main ingredients: confidence and pride in self, confidence and pride in leaders and confidence and pride in the team. From an army point of view, such a team might be the section, platoon, company, battalion, brigade or division.'[4]

This definition highlights two most essential elements for high morale: pride and confidence. Having confidence in his team and his leader is essential for someone to feel good and remain motivated. Pride comes from a sense of belonging and purpose. A man will never do anything until he finds a sense of purpose. In the armed forces, one 'feels' that he is fighting for a higher purpose. The military leadership, supported and backed by the rest of the nation, has to instil this sense of purpose in every soldier who fights for the country.

An American general defined morale as, '... a soldier thinks his army is the best in the world, his regiment the best in the army, his company the best in the regiment, his squad the best

---

[4]'Morale,' by Lieut.-Colonel J.G. Shillington, D.S.O., Journal of the Royal United Service Institution, Vol. XCV, February to November, 1950

in the company, and that he himself is the best blankety-blank soldier man in the outfit.'[5] This is an interesting definition as it is based on individual feeling and thoughts. If the soldier feels invincible, he becomes invincible for that moment. That is why there is so much emphasis on a sense of belonging, and in a subtle way, conveying: You belong to the best and you *are* the best.

According to Alexander H. Leighton, a sociologist and psychiatrist, 'Morale is the capacity of a group of people to pull together persistently and consistently in pursuit of a common purpose.'[6] In this case, emphasis on the 'pursuit of a common purpose'. It also implies that the purpose has to be worth the sacrifice. In this regard, Hitler made a strong case in front of the Germans. He made them believe that they were the best, the purest and the strongest race. This is how he wooed a nation of great scientists and musicians to fight against the world. He also gave them a purpose, convincing them to believe that the Treaty of Versailles was an unfair deal. A feeling of superiority and a strong purpose were enough to raise the morale of a nation that had been defeated in the previous war.

It Is Difficult to Quantify Morale

War is a strategy game. These strategies are created based upon simulated warlike situations to train military commanders in military operations at both the tactical and strategic levels, and are either drawn from real events or have fictitious settings.

---

[5] Knickerbocker, H.R. (2005). *Is Tomorrow Hitler's*? Kessinger Publishing.
[6] Leighton, A.H. (1949). *Human Relations in a Changing World: Observations on the Uses of the Social Sciences*.

There is an attempt to represent a reasonable approximation of the actual forces, terrain and other material factors faced by the real participants. The battlefield usually has two opposing forces pitted against each other, which are represented using sand models and maps or more recently, computer software. In such simulations, it is easy to depict and represent force levels, including military hardware and their lethality index, but it is very difficult to factor in morale. The reason is its intrinsically unquantifiable nature.

In his famous concept 'Fog of War', Clausewitz refers to certain properties that are unquantifiable and random in warfare and morale falls squarely into such a foggy domain. For morale, Lt Col. Daniel Smith, a military researcher, says that morale is 'a multifaceted concept and has many sides to it. Soldiers who fight for a cause must be convinced that the population of their country supports what they are doing. Do my countrymen, my leaders and my family care about me, respect me?' Here, morale is linked to the purpose and raison d'etre. The US Army Field Manual calls morale 'the human dimension's most important intangible element' and 'a measure of how people feel about themselves, their team and their leaders.' This definition again links morale to how an individual feels about his environment.

Importance of Morale for Decisive Victory: Morale as a Principle of War

Principles of war are those axioms that need to be kept in mind while planning and executing any military operation. These are universally accepted and self-evident truths. Around 500 BCE, Sun Tzu documented the earliest known and acknowledged military principles of war.

Dr John Alger defines principles as 'A fundamental truth that is professed as a guide to action.' By this definition, these become guiding principles for military commanders. These axioms are viewed as 'checks and balances' for operations planned at the tactical as well as strategic levels. These are usually 'in sync' with a nation's warfare doctrine and hence, most of the major powers have made their own principles. For instance, the US armed forces have agreed upon nine principles of war while the British have ten. Surprise, economy of effort and security are principles common to most of the nations.

General Eisenhower had said that morale, given a rough equality in other things, is supreme on the battlefield. General Montgomery, who fought many battles against the Germans during the Second World War, was of the opinion that there could be no compromise on the state of morale for the British troops, who were fighting the Axis powers against all odds in the North African campaign. During the Battle of El Alamein, he said, 'We must be very careful what we do with the British infantry. Their fighting spirit is based largely on morale and regimental esprit de corps. On no account must anyone tamper with this.'

Morale is not only applicable to military victory, but is also pivotal for a nation to remain united during a crisis, especially an all-out war. When a nation goes to war, it is not only the military that gets involved; the entire nation is at stake. After the Second World War, most of the wars were limited in nature, where participating belligerent nations did not commit their entire resources. Even in a limited war scenario, a nation does get impacted in terms of economy, petroleum resources and other material required in war. In such a scenario, the nation, as a whole, must back the war and be convinced that a conflict is warranted.

By the middle of 1943, Germans were losing on all fronts. Joseph Goebbels, the right-hand man of Adolf Hitler and propaganda minister in Hitler's regime, was finding it difficult to keep up the morale of the Germans. In an essay called 'Morale is the decisive force', dated 7 August 1943, he suggests that morale is the winning factor:

> We are in the midst of a decisive period in the war. Using unprecedented mass of weapons and psychological warfare, the enemy is attempting to capture positions that we won during the first half of this vast world struggle, and which are the foundation of our coming victory. The enemy hopes to achieve decisive breakthroughs on the front and also to shatter the morale of the German people. They hope to force us to our knees by massive attacks from all directions. The war against our nerves naturally has a critical role.

In 1940, the German Luftwaffe attacked only military and industrial targets, but the enemy's attacks today are directed almost exclusively against the civilian population and thereby, its morale.

> What we are experiencing in the air war is a test of nerves. The English withstood a test of nerves under less favorable political and military conditions in 1940; we must withstand it in 1943 [...] Much can be done by staying calm, being courageous and thinking clearly. Everyone needs to stay at his post and do his duty.
>
> The main burden of the war sometimes falls here,

other times there, and each must prove himself when it is his turn.

England has never won a war through a genuine military victory. It either sent other people to fight for it or it broke the nerve of its enemies even when there was no prospect of military success. It is trying it again with us. Our task is to frustrate the attempt.

During the Seven Year War, there were times when only the strength of its king rescued Prussia. Present crisis, is in no way, as severe as Prussia's. No one will be forgiven by posterity for failing under difficult circumstances. We will forget the difficulties as time passes. We will remember only the ways in which we overcame them.

The soldier at the front keeps his cool in critical situations, and when the order comes, he leaves his protecting trench to storm the enemy's position. If he does not, we call him a coward. Still, every attack demands courage, bravery, cold-bloodedness and a strong heart. We need these same virtues in the homeland with regards to morale, and if it comes to that, physically as well. Our troops in Sicily are fighting like the Devil, and that the attacker had to pay for every meter of ground with streams of blood. German sons stand at their distant posts and they prove through their unshakable heroism not only their physical, but also their moral courage. If our whole nation is filled with their spirit, the enemy can never defeat us.

The attacks of the enemy on our morale will fail in the face of our firm resolve, just as the storm of his weapons fail against the bravery of our front. We have become citizens of the world, and must behave accordingly.

Friend and foe alike look our way each day and ask: Will they pass the test?

Our war morale is a matter of the individual, but also of the community. It is attacked by the enemy today, and we must all defend it.

Morale Is a Leadership Function

The team captain, military commander or general are leaders entrusted with the responsibility of keeping the flag flying high and holding the hand of the team when the chips are down. One way or the other, all these people are responsible for the performance of their teams in action.

The captain of a cricket team, a shop floor manager in an automobile plant, the captain of a merchant vessel or a shift supervisor deep down in a coal mine are all 'men in charge' who need to get the work done from their teams and deliver the desired results. All of them are responsible for the behaviour and performance of their team members individually as well as collectively. All of them face challenges every day, the most challenging of which is to keep their teams in high spirits and even during the worst of the times, ensure that they deliver, and deliver well.

During a cricket match, when the going gets tough, the captain has to keep his cool and take the right decisions. If he panics, the team panics; it's that straight and simple. If there is an accident on the shop floor and a worker is fatally injured, the plant manager has to show restraint, take appropriate actions and keep the morale high. Similarly, during rough weather in choppy seas, it is the captain of the ship whom the crew looks up to for a safe sail through.

Major Arthur Harrison Miller, in his book *Leadership*, looks at morale a little differently. He establishes a link between leadership and morale in a scientific way and says that 'it is like a closed electrical circuit. Morale being the current, the powerful electromagnetic force and leadership is the conductor which guides the transmission of this force to the motor.'

> From the military leadership point of view, 'Leadership is the science of creating and maintaining high morale and directing it through action of men to achieve the result.' I would like to look at it a little more pragmatically and expand the above definition. In a battlefield and even before a battle has begun, 'Leadership is the generator of electromagnetic force and the desired current and thereafter provides a superconductivity to apply the current to the motor without any losses on the way!'

At the end of the day, it is the man on the ground who has to take the flag forward and lead his men to face the bullet. It is not merely a battle cry that creates the instant adrenaline rush making them move forward. People follow the leader because of the confidence built by the same leader over a period of time. This confidence constantly works at the back of the mind of every soldier and he knows that he has a good leader who will not fail him. He expects a commitment from his leader: 'Come what may, I will be with you always and every time.' Such confidence-building starts with peacetime training when a military leader demonstrates that he is good at his job; not only as good as them but better than them. A military leader, therefore, is in the field to participate in sports, he trains with them, he runs with them and he eats with them at appropriate occasions. Indirectly, he instils confidence in his men that during action, he would be able to lead them to victory. A military leader has to be physically as tough as his men. In addition, he is required to possess combat knowledge and skills more superior than the men he commands. Otherwise, his men will fail to follow him, especially in a crisis.

Unit cohesion is one major part of morale building. This means a sense of belonging, camaraderie, togetherness and solidarity. The lowest self-accounting unit is a company with over 100 men and the largest cohesive fighting formation is a corps with more than 100,000 men. Leaders at all levels need to emphasize that 'we are one unit and one people'. That is why units have their own insignias, symbols and distinct uniforms. The military uniform along with great leadership unifies the team members' minds and hearts. It is also very important to hold town hall meetings at all levels at regular intervals to allow steady contact and dialogue within the entire fighting force.

George Patton in his book *War As I Knew It*, written immediately after the Second World War in 1947, says,

> Officers are responsible, not only for the conduct of their men in battle, but also for their health and contentment when not fighting. An officer must be the last man to take shelter from fire and the first to move forward. Similarly, he must be the last man to look after his own comfort at the close of a march. He must see that his men are cared for. The officer must constantly interest himself in the rations of the men. He should know his men so well that any sign of sickness or nervous strain will be apparent to him, and he can take such action as may be necessary.

A well-fed, well-clothed and well-equipped army with adequate ammunition and support from the entire military establishment would possess high morale. Sound administration, therefore, is also a part of maintaining morale. This is also the responsibility of the leader. It is important to keep in touch with your men and to look after their needs. Taking care of every man under your command goes a long way in building this kind of trust.

The army, as a whole, is able to provide a sense of comfort and belonging that no other organization is able to provide. It is a seamless organization where a man from an entirely different unit or formation is welcomed with open arms into any of the units across the country. When good leadership is backed by a universally accepted ethos of brotherhood, it makes a great cohesive force that can withstand any calamity.

Esprit de Corps

Esprit de corps means a strong shared team spirit, sense of devotion and camaraderie. It is enshrined in most of the credos of military organizations. The credo of the National Defense Academy, where officers of the three services of Indian armed forces are trained, is 'Service Before Self.' The US Marine Corps demonstrates this spirit in its core values, 'Honour, Courage and Commitment.'

Pride and a sense of belonging are two strong components of espirit de corps. In teamwork, every team member is expected to become a part of the team and should be ready to accept what is good for the whole team and the mission. Esprit de corps goes a step ahead and is built upon the willingness to sacrifice oneself for the team and the mission. Such a level of commitment and sacrifice is seen only in the armed forces and rarely in any business organization. This is not surprising, because the men in uniform have a much higher purpose than a business organization, whose sole interest is commercial in nature. People join not-for-profit organizations to serve others and therefore demonstrate a much higher degree of team spirit. In other words, comfort and money cannot always be the driving force.

Another important point about esprit de corps is that it generates a feeling of 'one for all and all for one.' Consider one of the codes of conduct of the US Navy SEALS: 'I am ready for war. I will close and engage the enemy with the full combat power of my craft. My actions will be decisive yet measured. I will always complete the mission. *I will never quit and I will leave no one behind.*' Even the injured or dead will not be left behind. This is very reassuring and implies that one will never be abandoned, whatever the cost.

However, all this becomes very difficult in case an army is deployed to support some other distressed nation. In such a situation, a man may not be as motivated to deliver as he is on his own soil. Officers and soldiers both feel that it is someone else's war. Leaders on ground have to find ways and means to convince their teams of the purpose of their fight.

During the Second World War, the Americans were fighting in Europe for the British, the French and the rest of the European nations. Technically, the soldiers were not defending the sovereignty or soil of America. They were pushed into the fiercest of battles where more than a million American troops perished or were injured. As the war was coming to an end, Americans were advancing into German-occupied territory where they saw the horrors of concentration camps run by the Germans, the pathetic condition of the prisoners and how they had been reduced to skeletons in the ghettos. General George Patton himself took his men to show them the brutality of the

Germans and said, 'This is what we are fighting for.'

In the Mahabharata, as battle lines are drawn and both the armies stand against each other, Arjun, one of the Pandavas, mounts his chariot, sees his family and friends in the opposing army and is overcome with despair and disgust. He asks Krishna, 'How can I fight and kill my own brothers, uncles, teachers and friends?' Saying so, he casts away his bows and arrows and refuses to fight. Krishna, who is his charioteer, sees his predicament and says, 'Be courageous, pick up your weapon and go and destroy your opponent even if they are your family, because you are fighting for your right and a victory would mean the defeat of evil and restoration of the power of good.' Krishna precisely did what a leader should do in the heat of battle.

In their book *Built to Last*, Jim Collins and Jerry I. Porras have talked about companies whose top leadership was able to build morale and sustain the companies for decades just by defining goals that went beyond profit-making. Caring for your people, transparency and being honest and impartial are the factors that instil confidence in the team and take them towards a higher degree of commitment.

Words of Wisdom from War

Theoretical discussions and analysis of human behaviour under stress, especially during war, can never match the experiential learning of those who have been through it. It is difficult to imagine how people think and feel under such trying circumstances. It may look even more stupid and irrelevant if anyone would attempt to describe these situations theoretically.

During our academy days, we had several tactical exercises that involved long marches in the mountains, which required considerable stamina and determination. Each person had to carry a weapon, ammunition, blankets and rations and some clothing, which have to be used for several days. Therefore, everyone carries a considerably loaded backpack. It is also very cold and a bit of snowfall can make things worse. During one such expedition, it started raining heavily. Raincoats were of little help, as rainfall in these areas is accompanied with gushing winds that can even chill your marrow. We were a bunch of twenty cadets and were desperately looking for some shelter where we could spend the night. As soon as the scout spotted a small hutment, we all rushed in. It was a kind of ranch that was full of buffalos and cow dung. The place was so tiny that we were squeezed in like a tin of sardines. However, the only thing that mattered at that time was that it didn't rain inside! We were huddling together to generate body heat to feel somewhat cozy. Being together during such times is a great feeling, in terms of not only physical comfort but also as a psychological solace. We were so tired that within minutes, each one of us found a place and half the squad was snoring and sleeping right on top of the cow dung.

General Marshal in his book *Men Against Fire*, says,

> I hold it to be one of the simplest truths of war that the thing which enables an infantry soldier to keep going with his weapon is the near presence or the presumed presence of a comrade. The warmth, which derives from human companionship, is as essential to his employment of the arms with which he fights as is the finger with which he pulls a trigger or the eye with which he aligns his sights. The other man may be almost beyond hailing or seeing distance, but he must be there somewhere within

a man's consciousness or the onset of demoralization is almost immediate and very quickly the mind begins to despair or turns to thoughts of escape. In this condition, he is no longer a fighting individual.

Psyops Damage Morale; Not Tanks and Guns

In the initial days of the Second World War, the use of psychological operations (psyops) was amply demonstrated during the blitzkrieg unleashed by the Germans. They used Panzer tanks in concentrated formations to create shock and awe that was never witnessed before by either the French or the British.

Psyops or psychological warfare is known by different names like 'propaganda' and 'hearts and minds'. The major purpose of psyops is to demoralize the enemy forces and destroy their will to fight, so that the conflict is shortened and military and civilian casualties minimized on both sides. Psychological warfare is not only effective against soldiers and armies, but is also a potent weapon against governments and the civilian population. Armies alone do not fight a war; in a way, the whole nation gets involved. Since prehistoric times, demoralizing the enemy has been undertaken as a war technique. Alexander the Great influenced people in the conquered territories by leaving behind his men to spread Greek culture and marry locals to take them into his fold. He also inducted local chieftains into his administration to keep control of the conquered areas. In the 13th century, the generals of Genghis Khan would intimidate the people living in areas they wanted to occupy and many would submit without putting up a fight.

The Second World War witnessed the rapid development and deployment of organized psychological warfare and since then, every nation has made this a part of their war doctrine.

During the 1955 Vietnam War, Americans assassinated many National Liberation Front (NLF) personnel and terrorized its sympathizers, intimidating them to give up. They even encouraged defections. Around 20,000 NLF supporters were eliminated. This was called the Phoenix Program. During the 1991 Gulf War, leaflets were dropped to inform Iraqi soldiers that if they surrendered, they would be treated well, and there was no point fighting as they would lose the war any which way. As counter-psyops, Saddam Hussein tried to demoralize the American troops by telling them that while they were fighting in Iraq, their wives and girlfriends were being seduced by movie stars like Bart Simpson. In the 2003 invasion of Iraq, the American army successfully used 'shock and awe' tactics to maim the will of the Iraqi army. The firepower used was so huge that the enemy forces got scared and demoralized.

Modern Military Campaigns

Vietnam War (1955–1971)

The American army had been deployed in Vietnam primarily to contain communism in the region and support the democratic government. American troops were amongst the best, but the fighting force became demoralized very rapidly in this land war, which most Americans perceived as unnecessary. In 1971, the US Armed Forces Journal reported, 'The morale, discipline and battle worthiness of the US Armed Forces are lower and worse than at any time in this century.'

The top brass tried its level best to provide all the possible comfort to the troops including rest and relaxation breaks every one year to keep the morale high. Every amenity and comfort, which is humanly possible in combat conditions, was made available to the troop right at the front line. However, these did not give any worthwhile results. There were several reasons for this state of affairs. Firstly, at that point in time, the American youth was witnessing civil rights and women's liberation movements, and had tasted the fruits of affluence. There was turmoil within American society and the focus was on individual freedom and rights. They, therefore, were in no mood to fight a war that appeared to be pointless and with uncertain objectives.

The war was not a cakewalk. In Vietnam, a soldier had to go through hell in terms of harsh climate, unfamiliar terrain, marginal support from the local population and an invisible enemy who refused to give up. A substantial component of the American contingent comprised of soldiers hurriedly drafted and trained for this war. Young men were forced to enlist and those who refused were sentenced to jail. Neither were they extensively trained nor battle-hardened, and found it very difficult to remain motivated to fight. By 1969, they suffered a total breakdown of morale.

Soldiers saw themselves to be 'the unwilling, led by the unqualified, doing the unnecessary for the ungrateful.'[7] This was the mindset of a soldier in the thick of the battle. During the war, more than 9 million donned the uniform, and according to a study, 1,500,000 soldiers went AWL (Absent Without Leave) and more than 5,00,000 deserted. This is unthinkable for a

---

[7] Camp, N. M. (2014). *US army psychiatry in the Vietnam War: New challenges in extended counterinsurgency warfare.* Government Printing Office.

professional army. There were widespread mutinies and cases where unpopular and strict officers were killed by their own soldiers. The overall turmoil and rebellion in the American society reflected on the armed forces on the battleground. Cases of drug and alcohol abuse reached unprecedented levels and more than 50 per cent soldiers were engaged in anti-war dissent. This came to be known as the GI Movement.

It was a humiliating defeat for the US and taught a lesson to the top military and political brass to reshape the armed forces as a volunteer organization rather than based on forced conscription.

Operation Desert Storm (August 1990–January 1991)

In 1990, the US waged a war against Saddam Hussein's regime in response to Iraq's invasion of Kuwait. Popularly known as Operation Desert Storm, it was a coalition force of 34 nations led by the Americans. Immediately after the invasion of Kuwait by Iraqi forces, there were protests and several demonstrations by the Iraqi public, which was not in favour of the war. The prices of commodities like food and other essentials had become more than twenty times. There were large-scale desertions in the Iraqi army despite a 200 per cent hike in salaries.

The Americans wanted to avoid a land war and desired to pulverize the Iraqi morale by massive air bombardment. This began on 17 January 1991 and continued for five weeks. There were more than 1,000 sorties every day, which primarily pounded Iraqi military targets and radar stations. The most advanced weapon systems were deployed and used for maximum affect. Precision-guided munitions, cluster munitions and cruise missiles were used to demoralize the

Iraqi public as well as army. After five weeks, on 24 February, the coalition forces launched a massive ground attack to drive out the Iraqi forces from Kuwait and advanced into Iraqi territory. Within 100 hours, the coalition forces declared a ceasefire.

The air raids had had a chilling effect on the Iraqi army; almost 40 per cent of the Iraqi army had deserted and the ones still holding out had little will to fight. There were more desertions than deaths, which ultimately depleted the strength of Saddam's army. Across the war theatre, the coalition army felt that the low morale of the Iraqi army was the single most important reason for their quick victory. Several Iraqi units felt they were defeated even before the battle had begun. Even the Americans had not expected such a massive breakdown of Iraqi morale, because of their experience in the Second World War and Vietnam.

Building and Maintaining the Morale of a Fighting Force

There is no one rule of thumb that can work to keep up the morale of a fighting force. It requires constant and consistent effort using multiple methods simultaneously. All these methods aim at building cohesion, camaraderie, pride, a sense of purpose, belonging, bonding and solidarity. One's morale automatically gets boosted when all these factors are taken care of.

Training and discipline are on top of the stack. Collective training and tactical exercises, simulating a warlike scenario, instilling confidence and inculcating brotherhood amongst a large fighting force builds that martial spirit. A well-disciplined force is less likely to get demoralized easily.

The military uniform is another great way to create a sense

of cohesiveness. It brings uniformity and a sense of similarity. An individual identifies himself with this huge organization called the armed forces. A smart uniform, which a man must be proud of wearing, can go a long way in building individual pride. This may also instil a sense of being more able than their civilian counterparts.

A well-turned-out soldier, eating in a proper mess and living in a healthy and clean environment, feels good about himself and his organization. This instils camaraderie and pride. Cantonments across the world are, thus, well maintained.

Medals and ribbons also have a special place in the heart of a soldier, as morale, pride, sacrifice and honour are exhibited by them. That is why they wear these medals at all times. The Indian Param Vir Chakra and Maha Vir Chakra, the German Iron Cross, the British Victoria Cross, and the American Medal of Honour and Purple Heart are lifetime achievement awards for men in uniform.

Martial tunes are also great motivators. These tunes are played by military bands with much pomp and show, and this helps in pepping up the morale of every individual.

A soldier is motivated by words like 'duty', 'honour', 'service' and 'pride'. These are not mere words, and they impact one's morale positively. Along with these, symbolic gestures towards the men in uniform need to be made from time to time as well. A soldier should never feel that he has been shortchanged or taken for granted by his unit, countrymen or nation. Upgradation of salaries from time to time, and looking after the administrative needs of every individual, like his housing, clothing, food and family, are the important yet necessary needs that must be met. During the Second World War and even till a few decades later, morale was not linked to monetary compensations or materialistic comforts. A soldier was happy with his plight and took pride in his hardships and the sacrifice he made. That was the difference between a mercenary and a soldier: while one fought for money, the other fought for his honour and country. Even today, this is true to a large extent, but society is fast becoming materialistic and change is inevitable. Taking this cue, some modern armies look after the soldiers in such a way that it may look like 'pampering' to any other person. A soldier is not only looked after during peacetime, but also during the operations where maximum efforts are made to provide every possible facility.

How to Factor in Morale in the Context of Civilian Organizations

Morale is a word used typically in the context of the armed forces. In a civilian setup, more often than not, one talks about motivation. If organizations can learn from the ethos of the armed forces and try to look at their people as 'one whole', a lot can be achieved. If this is done, we will be able to create a workforce and an organization par excellence. The difference between morale and motivation, and the latter's effective usage in organizations that work for profit, are mentioned below:

What Is Morale?

Morale is the collective feeling of a group as a whole and is related to how people collectively perceive their leadership, group dynamics, a particular situation/event and the organization they work for. It is important for each individual in the group to be convinced that he is working for something worthwhile. It is also about a sense of belonging. Morale, therefore, is the perception of a group, which eventually affects the mental state of every individual in that group. If the morale of the organization is high, it will help motivate every individual.

Another important attribute of morale is the performance of the group as a collective entity. It is the excellence of the entity and not only of an individual that boosts morale. For instance, in a football match, the coach or the captain looks at the team as 'one entity' when it performs or perishes. The performance of the centre forward or goalkeeper is secondary. A military commander also views his unit or his formation in the same 'gross' way.

Morale, therefore, acquires primary importance in organizations that are team driven and are viewed as cohesive entities. Unfortunately, in business organizations, the motivation of an individual acquires primary concern. The focus, therefore, is to keep every individual happy, motivated and committed. He should be largely committed to himself, his performance, his goals, his targets, his progress, his promotion and his take-home pay. If these are satisfied, the focus and commitment will shift to the organization and the team will automatically perform better.

What Does Motivation Entail?

A motivated person demonstrates the drive, enthusiasm and inspiration to perform, coupled with self-confidence and dedication to *his* work. It is related to an individual's performance and his own satisfaction with the job or his compensation. Every individual can be motivated if his individual interests are taken care of. The organization needs to address his personal problems, job-related issues or welfare concerns. Since this is incentive-driven, better rewards will be a driving factor.

What Does Morale Entail?

Morale is related more to the intangibles. It is gotten by pride, respect, spirit, sacrifice, honour, purpose, a sense of belonging and the collective good, victory and camaraderie. Attending a workshop on motivation may inspire someone to do well at an individual level and make him the best performer in the company, but it will not be able to instil pride or a feeling of affiliation with the organization he works for. Unfortunately, the corporate world has mostly missed this salient feature of human excellence.

Focus on Morale

- **Organizations need to focus on building a sense of belonging among the people who work there.** A person should no longer work for himself alone, but also work with a purpose for the collective good. Organizations should be able to articulate their raison d'etre convincingly. Every organization should exist for something besides profit making. If you can identify that 'something' and put it in simple words, you are moving in the right direction.
- **Build an organization into an honourable brand** that is respected and has a name that people would like to associate with. A company can create a working philosophy that is appealing, meaningful and genuinely good. People should be proud to work for that name because it stands for something—quality, integrity, philanthropy. The purpose could be caring for the nation, environment, etc., but it should be bigger than the organization itself.

- Several organizations focus on team work and take employees for out-of-office activities to **inculcate team spirit**. These activities foster camaraderie, and spending money and time on these will pay rich dividends. In the armed forces, there is a lot of emphasis on 'troop games' where officers and team members play together. Football, hockey, basketball and volleyball are some of the popular ones. Officers play individual games like squash, tennis or golf too, but are encouraged to play troop games.

Startups work against all odds, and are like newly born children who are yet to learn how to take their first step. The founders often invest their hard-earned savings and are not even sure when they would be able to see the light at the end of the tunnel, working with little finance and a very small team. These often affect the team members' motivation levels.

The first 1,000 days of a new business are very tough and one has to fight against all odds to survive. This is like a battlefield scenario, where the leader has to show courage and grace under pressure. It is not simple, but those who can do it are able to retain their teams. Employees have to be taken into confidence and often need to be told the reality. It is better to be transparent, because that earns you trust and that is all you have in such a situation. Once the initial struggle is over, the business grows very fast. This is the time to build a good culture. Remember, a new organization doesn't have to unlearn anything since it has no past. Therefore, at this nascent stage, the founders must pay attention to building a value system, a sense of belongingness and team spirit. A similar situation occurs when new units are raised in the army. The manpower is pooled in from different units and initially there is no cohesion. The equipment, ammunition and vehicles also get pooled in and trickle in one by one. This is the time when the commanding officer has to demonstrate maturity and patience. From the time a unit is raised, effort must be put in to build a sense of camaraderie and team spirit. The officers have to ensure that their men feel that they belong to an organization that will care for them.

Maslow's hierarchy defines five levels of human need. The lowest being the physiological, which takes care of basic existence. The next level being security, which every organization takes care of by giving adequate compensation and benefits. The third level is 'love and belonging' and this is where organizations can play a big role. This sense of belongingness is all about camaraderie and esprit de corps. The fourth level is about an individual's esteem. This is where respect and the feeling of belonging to an elite organization or a fighting group, as in the armed forces, come into play. Recognitions, ribbons, awards, shields and trophies have their own charm and impact. While level two deals with motivation at an individual level, organizations must take care of levels three and four, which concern morale.

They must have frequent town hall meetings and communicate with people at all levels. Leaders must work along with their team members as much as possible. Unfortunately, electronic connectivity has severed face-to-face connections, and most of the top echelon communicates only through these means. Moving out of your cabin to other floors and having regular interaction helps foster great bonds and a sense of confidence.

Being hands-on can establish you as a great leader and will change the way the group you lead perceives you. For example, in the middle of the night, if there is an accident in a plant and there are a couple of people seriously injured, what should be the action of the managing director of the company? Does his duty finish by taking a report on the phone sitting at home, announcing some ex gratia payment and telling someone to escort them to the hospital? Technically yes, but from the leadership point of view, a little more is expected. If the man reaches the spot immediately, it will raise the morale of the workers. The leader will not only motivate the injured individually by his actions, but also raise the morale of the entire unit by that one visit. He will have proved that 'no one will be abandoned'. He would also have given 'respect' to every man on the shop floor, thereby earning their loyalty.

3

Blitzkrieg: Lightning Warfare

'Lead me, follow me or get the hell out of my way.'
—George S. Patton

Mobile Warfare Over the Centuries

Speed and strength have always been the most important aspects of winning in combat. Therefore the horse, which is one of the most agile animals, had been extensively used in wars for more than 300,000 years, for example in the Mughal period, for Napoleonic wars, European campaigns as well as the American Civil War.

In the last couple of centuries, organized military forces that fought on horseback were designated as cavalry. They were extensively used during the First World War and to a limited extent during the Second World War as well. Wherever cavalry was used, it attacked with speed and force and created fear in the minds of infantry soldiers. This is how mobile warfare was conducted before mechanical transport became feasible.

Trench Warfare

Trench warfare was a new war strategy that changed the complexion of warfare entirely. Troops occupied trenches that protected them from firing by small arms and also from bombing by artillery guns. Both sides dug up trenches and this was a sure recipe for a long-drawn stalemate. Since machine guns had come on the scene, horses and horsemen could be easily mowed down by a machine gun which could fire 400 to 600 rounds per minute. Barbed wires and obstacles also protected the trenches and the cavalry could not launch an attack, making mobile warfare as good as redundant.

A wonder weapon was needed to break this stalemate. Something was required that could breach through the barbed wires and other man-made obstacles and go over the trenches. The British came up with a solution and invented the tank.

Beginning of Mechanized Warfare

Before the tank was fully developed, armoured cars came on the scene, but they lacked maneuverability in rough terrain. Continuous or chain tracks gave tanks great cross-country mobility. Though their combat value became immediately apparent to military leaders, the number of tanks available on the battlefield was very few and there was no opportunity to develop any tactics to use them on a large scale.

By the beginning of the Second World War however, warfare became a game of fast maneuverability with tanks, APCs, self-propelled artillery guns and air-borne firepower all clubbed together. During a period of just 20 years, i.e. 1919–39 (between the two world wars), substantial development happened in the field of aviation, weapon technology and communication technology. A new breed of tanks and weapons were now available to military commanders, which, if used properly, could make a difference. During that time, the technology available to most nations was very much the same, and therefore, the weapon systems also had almost similar capabilities, thus putting most of them on a level playing field. Since the capabilities were almost at par, the only way to defeat the adversary was by having an overwhelming superiority of numbers. The second and more important factor was to use these numbers for maximum effect.

Military strategy was going to play a much more important role than it ever did before. At the end of the First World War, the tank was seen as a replacement of the horse in moving along with the infantry and giving it adequate support and protection. Not surprising then, some of the cavalry units retained their old names and armoured regiments and were still called the Second Lancers, the 3 Cavalry or the 17 Horse. Collectively, a tank force was called the armoured corps.

Developing New Doctrines of Armoured Warfare

At the beginning of the Second World War, the major adversaries were the British and the Germans, as America joined the war much later. To start with, the British had more number of tanks than the Germans, and also had better tanks in terms of speed and firepower. But even with a superior tank force, they were unable to use tanks as a force multiplier. The British and French both allotted few tank units to formations and, in a way, 'thinned out' the armoured resources. They were used more in a supportive role and deployed according to the infantry divisional commander's requirement.

The Germans, on the other hand, had realized the potential of this war machine and wanted to use this as a 'decisive force.' They combined armoured units to create armoured brigades, armoured divisions and full-fledged armoured corps. At the beginning of the Second World War, in September 1939, German armoured divisions had 300 to 350 tanks, which could be used as one cohesive force and deliver a massive punch to the enemy defenses. While investing heavily in tank technology, Germans created a tank called Tiger I, their most formidable piece of armour with an 88-mm main gun. Most British tanks had a 75-mm gun throughout the war. German tanks also had an edge in terms of speed.

Gradually, German generals and planners realized that tanks should become the striking force, supported by air power, infantry, artillery and even para-dropped soldiers where required. However, coordinating such a large number of mobile elements across a battlefield was the major hurdle.

Blitzkrieg: A New Strategic Initiative

During the Second World War, General Guderian was chief of the German mobile forces and was the brain behind the German armour warfare initiative. The German Panzer forces consisting of Panzer tanks were raised and organized under his guidance. He developed this concept and discussed it in detail in his book *Panzer Leader*. The main idea that he put forth was a combined all-arms tactic, where the infantry would be mounted on armoured vehicles and move along at the same speed as the tanks. This was later called 'matching mobility'. He conducted many mock exercises and sand model discussions to validate this concept. By 1930, he was convinced that for a decisive victory, tanks needed support from all other forces, like the infantry, artillery and even air power. He turned the entire concept of conducting warfare on its head, because till now, the rest of the major armies were using tanks to support infantry and other arms. He created tank formations and brought all other weapons and forces under the command of these armoured formation commanders.

Guderian also realized that an excellent intra- and inter-system communication was required to coordinate so many elements. By then, radio and wireless communication technology had arrived and he wanted more R&D in this field. Very soon, every German tank had a couple of radio sets to communicate with the rear as well as the front. German tank commanders were in a much better position to manoeuvre their tanks than the Allied forces.

The Basic Principles of Lightning Warfare

'Scherpunktprinzip' is a German principle of concentration, which is similar to 'all hands on deck.' Every single element of the military force was put to use in a blitzkrieg attack, with each element having a very specific role to play.

Germans referred to the centre of gravity as 'schwerpunkt', a focal point and the point of maximum impact. It is very much akin to the effect a laser beam has, or a lens that captures sunrays and concentrates the entire energy at a focal point to burn it out. Guderian summarized the effect of this concept by defining it as *'Klotzen nicht kleckern,'* which means 'Boot them, don't spatter them,' because the strike was concentrated and not dispersed, and acted like a hard kick. This idea of the focal point was drilled into every soldier.

Three camaraderie-related points were also impressed upon the entire rank and file of this mobile force. A sense of belonging, mutual trust and being part of an elite group were together referred to by the Germans as 'einheit'. This was also to provide a psychological comfort to an individual, indicating that he could fully depend on his team members, including his superiors. Germans also built an awe-inspiring relation between the superior and the subordinate by building a code of conduct. Superiors were expected to know what their subordinates were capable of and accordingly give orders to accomplish a task. Thereafter, it was left to the subordinate to complete the task. No micromanagement was required and the subordinate also appreciated not being asked to do something that he was not capable of. This was like an operational contract between a subordinate and his superior and was known as 'auftragstaktik'.

The entire rank and file was motivated to feel that they were the best and through several rigourous training sessions, each member was made to understand that nobody could perform better than them. This intuitive skill was termed as 'fingerspitzengefuhl'.

Surprise was the major element for success. The final hour and the point of attack would never be known to the enemy who was kept on his toes and didn't know where he would be hit. The French and the British responded piecemeal and never brought a counterattack as one cohesive strike.

The focal point was to make a 'hole' in the enemy defense. This was achieved by an armoured attack, backed by a motorized infantry (now called mechanized infantry), artillery fire and air bombardment. Even if the attacker was inferior in number, a breach could be created due to this hole, through which tanks and mechanized infantry could pass. Air support played an important role to pulverize the enemy. The breakout operation led tanks to fan out into the enemy areas, and not allowing them to organize a counter-attack. Despite having very good communications, decentralized mission-oriented orders were disseminated to the lowest level of leadership, where commanders would take decisions as they deemed fit. It was 'aufragstaktik', or leadership from the front all the way. The mop-up operation to destroy pockets of enemy forces left along the flanks was done by specific elements that came in from the rear and inflicted heavy causalities on a bewildered enemy. It was here that maximum damage was done to the enemy forces. The Germans' strategy proved that the small could indeed beat the big with speed and concentration.

The Underestimation of German Tactics by the Allies

During September 1939, German forces started the Second World War by attacking Poland. That is the time when they unleashed their tank force in an organized manner on Europe, lashing this fist of fury across France. This Blitzkrieg brought them quick success. They swept across Poland in 26 days, with the Baltic States surrendering in less than a week, Denmark falling in four hours and the French armies defeated in just five weeks. The British were saved because of the English Channel, which acted like a natural obstacle and a buffer between them and the German armies.

The British had underestimated the German war machine. On 19 May 1940, Winston Churchill said, 'It would be foolish to disguise the gravity of the hour. It would be still more foolish to lose heart and courage or to suppose that well-trained and well-equipped armies numbering three or four million men can be overcome in the space of a few weeks, or even months, by a scoop or raid of mechanized vehicles, however formidable. We may look with confidence to the stabilization of the front in France.' Even someone as well-informed as Churchill was unable to understand the fact that a blitzkrieg could achieve what they believed was impossible. Thirty-two days later, in the same rail road car and at the same place where Germany had signed the unconditional surrender in 1918, Adolf Hitler accepted the defeat and surrender of France.

In the 1940s in North Africa, Field Marshal Erwin Rommel,

using the same technique with his armoured field force, delivered a crushing defeat to the well-trained professional British army.

Blitzkrieg as a Concept in Modern-Day Warfare

This war technique has been repeated by some of the most advanced armies in today's time, and the concept will also be used in the future. For a quick and decisive battle, a strategy similar to blitzkrieg is essential even today. No country can afford a prolonged war due to the massive expenses. Speed and concentration of force are as important as they were during the Second World War. In fact, these two elements have become much more relevant today due to tremendous improvement in weapon systems and the mobility of troops. Communication has become as good as foolproof. Therefore, mobility, firepower and coordination have become decisive pivots in modern warfare.

During the Gulf War, which lasted close to seven months (2 August 1990–28 February 1991), the culminating Operation Desert Storm finished the war in just one month and twelve days. The battle began with a massive US-led air offensive, which wiped out Iraq's oil refineries, weapon plants, communication networks and radar establishments. They used all the latest technologies like stealth bombers, smart bombs, cruise missiles and laser-guided weapons. The air force of Iraq was reduced to a few aircraft as most others were destroyed on the ground itself. Operation Desert Storm created such 'shock and awe' that it resulted in panic among the Iraqi rank and file. Around 15 February, the air power was diverted to destroy Iraqi ground forces in Southern Iraq and Kuwait. Achieving total air superiority over the Iraqi air force, the coalition forces began their ground offensive, demolishing Iraq's armoured capability. As an estimate, the coalition forces lost only 300 troops whereas Iraqi forces lost around 10,000 men.

The Fundamental Principles of Lightning Warfare

- **Planning and preparedness:** Detailed planning, mock drills and rehearsals are crucial for the success of any large-scale operation.
- **Detailed orders to be passed on to the smallest units in advance:** This is to ensure that junior commanders can seize opportunity in a rapidly moving operation, where there is little time to pass orders.
- **Surprise is very important**: Secrecy and stealth are the keys to success.
- **Use of overwhelming local superiority:** At the focal point, the use of maximum effort is essential.
- **Attack is the best form of defense:** Therefore, seize initiative.
- **Create a psychological impact:** Use methods to 'shock and awe' the enemy so that they lose their nerve and morale.
- **Use of enemy resources:** Once the enemy areas are captured, it is important to capture all his resources like fuel, food and shelter and use them for your own forces.
- **Plan logistics well in advance:** Food and fuel must keep pace with that of warfare.
- **Don't worry about flanks**: This is imperative, though separate mop-up teams must destroy the remaining enemy forces after the mechanized forces have moved ahead.

- Dos and Don'ts:
  i. *Don't*
     - make mid-course corrections, unless absolutely necessary, as they can be disastrous.
     - bite more than what you can chew; know your limitations.
     - neglect your logistics.
     - let the enemy reorganize.
  ii. *Do*
     - have strong communication lines.
     - pool all resources.
     - use technology to its optimum.
     - remember that being fast is important.
     - keep space for flexibility, which should be built into the plan.
     - pass detailed orders in the beginning.

Blitzkrieg in a Changing World Order

In the last quarter of a century, the way business is done has considerably changed. There are basically two major reasons for this dramatic change—first, political, and second, rapid changes in technology.

After the Second World War, the world order changed with the US and the Union of Soviet Socialist Republics (USSR) dominating the world militarily and, hence, politically. During this period, which lasted 46 years (1945-91), there was a Cold War between the Americans and the Soviets, with many claiming an American domination of the world even then. The year 1991 was a watershed year that yet again redefined the world political order. With USSR disintegrating, the US emerged as the de facto 'superpower'. This did not last long, as several regional powers emerged, making the world a multi-polar planet. This was the new world order, along with which emerged the new world economic order that impacted nation states, their economies and also the way trade was done amongst nations.

Almost in the same time frame, a new world technological order appeared. It literally broke political and economic barriers. It ushered in speed and opportunity. Worldwide connectivity and great communications were the result of cutting edge technology, which developed extremely fast over the last two decades.

British economist Frances Cairncross in her 1997 book *The Death of Distance* talks of the social and economic effects of the global communications revolution. A decade and a half later, telematics, a fine blend of computers and communications, added another dimension to business and social order. It is now more to do with 'the death of time' than distance. Killing distance has made things easier, though the death of time is creating stress, as the time for battlefield commanders and business leaders to react is getting highly compressed. Leaders need to be mentally agile to survive in such a demanding scenario.

The turnaround time for any business transaction has been compressed manyfold. This age of opportunity has raised individual aspirations. 'Yes I can' has become an individual's war cry. It has also created fierce competition. Though markets have swelled and margins dipped, the window of opportunity has also shrunk. If a new technology or an opportunity appears, you need to go for the kill immediately and in a big way, because many would be waiting and watching out for this moment. Business has become like a war and product launches, project management, marketing campaigns and advertising are all individual battles.

Agility of Thought: Responsiveness

In a book titled *It's Not the Big that Eat the Small...It's the Fast that Eat the Slow*, authors Jason Jennings and Laurence Haugton argue that the world's most successful companies that surged ahead within their business vertical were the ones who chose to move at a dizzying speed. Hotmail, started by Indian entrepreneur Sabeer Bhatia, zoomed to bag $400 million from Microsoft in about two years of its existence. You not only have to think fast but also act fast. One needs to develop the reflexes of a fighter pilot, in thought as well as action.

Learning from experience is also very important. Germans learnt a lot from their defeat in the First World War. While the British, French and even the Americans used new weapons in the same way, the Germans used them to their advantage by creating a new paradigm of manoeuvre warfare.

Similarly, though new technologies are now available to all, many are doing business much the same way as they did earlier. New technologies as powerful as Enterprise Resource Planning, the Internet, cloud computing, social media, etc. not only offer new business opportunities, but also help us reorganize the way we do our existing business. For instance, cloud computing allows the sharing of virtual computing power. One can therefore get floating computing power, which can be scaled up or scaled down as per demand. In addition, it allows an organization to move from a capital expense model to an operational expense model, by sharing a common cloud infrastructure—you pay as you use, thereby avoiding upfront infrastructure cost. Hundreds of such new innovative technologies, big and small, are emerging every day. Business leaders who can appreciate these and best adapt to them will be the winners.

Dealing with the Changing Environment: Blitzkrieg Philosophy

The world is becoming smaller and flatter, and at the same time, less stable economically as well as politically.

The German strategy of blitzkrieg was to attack and defeat a known opponent in a known territory. Therefore mobile warfare characterized by speed, power, concentration of resources, flexibility and surprise could work very well. The blitzkrieg philosophy can be applied to businesses where there are defined adversaries or competition. For instance, if there are two existing cellular service providers in a telecom circle, the third entrant to that circle has a well-defined competition. They know who they are pitched against. Similarly, the majority of business situations will be 'one on one' type. In such a hostile environment, a rapid action plan consisting of an extremely agile marketing strategy, blazing advertisements, branding and well-thought-out penetrating pricing will be akin to a blitzkrieg.

Change being the only constant today, blitzkrieg thinking can also be of great help to handle this ever-changing business environment. A blitzkrieg mindset with adequate resources can be a game changer in order to deliver a rapid response to sporadic or even erratic change. Today, our real adversary in business is not another company, but the uncertainty—of a changing environment, policies and fiscal changes that impact our existing business and future expansion plans. To respond to such rapid changes, the organization must be able to act, almost in near real-time.

In today's warfare however, the blitzkrieg may not work in its original avatar in many situations because the war scenario has changed. Today we witness limited wars, contained within small geographical areas and fought often only along the borders of warring nations. Deep penetration using conventional warfare is usually never undertaken. In addition to terror warfare, insurgency is on the rise and has become a worldwide menace. Today, armies and security forces are fighting a 'faceless enemy', whose identity, and many times even purpose, is not clearly established. One cannot use tank and air warfare against an enemy that quickly melts into the air. Instead, technology is used to keep a tab on such terrorist organizations, their hideouts and their designs. Rapid action groups are created and kept ready to move, on very short notice, to deliver a near-real-time response.

Applying Lightning Warfare to Business

Business leaders who would like to optimize their resources and take the changing business scenario head-on must keep the basic principles of blitzkrieg in mind. Remember, in an all-out business war, your competition is your enemy, and you, as the CEO/leader, would be the commander.

- **When to use?**: You must first decide which of your projects or situations need a blitzkrieg response, because this would require your entire attention and massive resources. It is not required in any and every situation. Assess your priorities and then take a call.
- **Calling all stations**: Once you have decided to launch

the blitzkrieg, you need to have 100 per cent resources committed for deployment. Remember scherpunktprinzip, the principle of concentration? Your manpower, systems and machinery must move in the same direction to achieve the same goal. Each department must be in sync with and in support of others for this lightning strike, quite like the air support, artillery and tanks in a battle.

- **Never allow the enemy to counter-attack**: Speed and accuracy are paramount. Hence, the entire team, however large, must be briefed in advance and work with clockwork precision. Always remain ahead of your competition and 'keep on rolling'. Never halt. You must remain one step ahead in innovation, ideas and products so that you are never caught off-guard.
- **Best boys on deck**: The strike corps or the strike formation in war has the best equipment and best men. The strike unit commanders are always handpicked. Do the same in your business if you have a do-or-die situation. In business, where you have to win, whatever the odds, call upon your best managers, engineers and associates to rally together. Get your first string workers, or the A team, best technology and even the best consultants. You should not settle for anything less and then you can launch a lightning attack. You also need to have the necessary approvals in place so that there is no ambiguity at the time of execution. Get your necessary sanctions from the top management in advance, so that you are never left in the lurch.

During the Second World War in the North African campaign, Adolf Hitler had sent one of his best blitzkrieg commanders, General Erwin Rommel. The idea was to defeat the British totally and establish control over the entire Middle East. But he did not support him fully as initially planned. In May 1942, the Africa corps led by Rommel staged a full-fledged blitzkrieg attack on the British forces, which started retreating in big numbers. To defeat the British totally, Rommel required significant reinforcements and supplies. Hitler refused as he wanted to keep resources for the offensive in Russia. Just to teach Stalin a lesson, he let go of the strategically important Egypt, which at that point, would have been very easy for Rommel to capture. The British quickly capitalized on this blunder, and attacked the German forces, inflicting heavy casualities. In his personal diary, Rommel later wrote, 'Supplies and material are decisive in modern warfare. For my army, catastrophe was looming on the distant horizon. The British got their supplies and fresh troops, ruining our only chance to win the battle.'

Modify the Template: Create Your Own Execution Style

This is the most important aspect for the success of an operation. Never copy, but instead create your own methods. It is always good to learn from history and other leaders, but ultimately you need to fight your own battle, your own way. Modify the strategy as per your needs, create that shock and awe among your competitors and let them get surprised with your every move, your every product and your every launch. As people remember great generals like Rommel and Guderian, your decisive and creative strategies shall be remembered in the years to come. The ones that demonstrate brilliance could even become business case studies.

Auto Pilot

Never forget fingerspitzengefuhl, i.e. to create a sense of being the best amongst your team members because you plan, and ultimately they deliver. Create that invisible bond of auflragstaktik between the supervisors/managers and their teams to enhance confidence and a sense of belonging.

Your system should be so perfected, executions so well-rehearsed and instructions so detailed that your organization should work on autopilot. Only if major defaults occur during execution should the flag be raised for your intervention. Spend money on training, automation, standard operating procedures and above all, perfect documentation.

Corporate Scenarios Best Suited for Blitzkreig

In today's business scenario, speed and quick responses are required for almost any and every situation. Therefore, a lightning action may be applicable in most cases.

Corporate Turnaround

A quick decisive action with surgical precision could best work for a company that is not doing well and needs to get into shape. Kewal Nohria became the CEO of Crompton Greaves in 1985, when the company was in a bad shape. It was one of the leading electrical engineering companies and had manufacturing plants in multiple locations but Nohria was convinced that they were overstaffed and the workers underperformed, and went in for a total restructuring while working on total quality management. He said, 'The wind had abruptly changed direction and my job was to set the sails right again and correct the course.'

Nohria noticed that the production department decided what was to be made and asked the marketing staff to get orders for that. He reversed that immediately, with the production department taking inputs from the marketing team, which received their information directly from customer interaction. Within a year, the production plants had 21,000 kaizens, the highest number in the country.

The entire top management was involved and Nohria enjoyed the confidence of the senior management and had their total approval. The overhaul of inventory control was carried out with new production methods and the technology was upgraded. Just-in-time inventory was provided and cross-functional teams were formed to solve problems instantly. Instead of firing the extra staff, he redeployed them elsewhere, thus taking the entire labour force along the path of efficiency and commitment. Within a few years, the company turnover as well as individual productivity doubled, profits increased by six times and the efficiency of the company went up by 51 per cent.

Corporate Takeovers

A corporate takeover is well planned, deliberate, well devised, and most of the times, secretive. Almost all hostile takeovers are similar to a blitzkrieg. Speed and surprise are very important so that existing management and manpower does not get time to react. The new staff moves in quickly and any internal resistance is dealt with firmly.

Marketing Campaign

Take the instance of American grooming company Old Spice, which created a new brand ambassador, Mr Wolfdog, in 2015, and extensively hammered this new mascot for one week across all available media channels like Twitter, Google, YouTube, Facebook, Tumbler, Instagram and Bandcamp. In just one week, it raked in 44 million video and 600,000 website views. The company followed the three basic principles of blitzkrieg: come up with an idea (disruption) that was a disturbance for the consumers; keep moving nonstop across all channels; and use the best resources/channels of communication.

In the current marketing, advertising and branding scenario, there is so much competition and clutter in the media space that one has to have deep pockets to make noise and then be heard by one's customer. The only way to survive in this chaos is a short 'burst' of your message pushed over a reasonably long time, which can bombard the minds of your customers several times in that period, so as to create brand retention in their mind. If you have limited resources, do not disperse them across a large area. Follow the principle of concentration of force. If you deploy your smaller resources in a smaller area, you will be able to easily make a hole or an effective dent. Similar action can then be replicated in different geographical territories.

The blitzkrieg technique, intelligently modified to suit one's requirement, can be a winner, hands down.

4

Force Multipliers: The Game Changers

> '*Whoever said the pen is mightier than the sword obviously never encountered automatic weapons.*'
>
> —Douglas MacArthur

Force multiplication is a military term that refers to a combination of methodologies, applied in unison, which can enhance the effect of an existing military force without increasing its strength. For instance, if the use of radio communication in tank warfare can enhance the fighting capacity of an armoured formation by, say, three times, then radio communication technology becomes a force multiplier and the multiplication factor is three. The cost of a force multiplier is justified by the multiplication factor it can yield. Higher the multiplication factor, the better it is, as that can dramatically increase the effectiveness of a military force. Viewed as a game changer by modern armies over the years, it has brought about a paradigm shift in military affairs and warfare. Technology and certain critical inventions have been the biggest contributors towards force multiplication, thereby making the existing military capability of a country much more potent and lethal.

Such technology-enabled support systems create a virtual force that is more than an actual force. To give an analogy, a loudspeaker's output is usually linked to its physical volume—bigger the speaker, bigger the sound. Using certain methods, however, the volume of a box can be increased and even a much smaller speaker can be made capable of delivering sound that is as much as the sound delivered by a large speaker.

Going back to history, it was almost 150 years ago when Carl Von Clausewitz, the German Prussian military theorist, proposed the doctrine of force multiplier. He said that a small advantage in manpower and firepower (weapons) can give a huge advantage to an army.

For instance, if Army X has 2 units and Army Y has 3 units then Army Y has an advantage of $3^2 - 2^2$, which is 5 times.

If Army Y has 6 units as against 2 of X's, the advantage to Y is $6^2 - 2^2 = 32$ times.

Force multiplication, therefore, has an exponential effect on the outcome. In the last 100 years, several new ideas, tools, weapons and ground realities have been used by armies innovatively in order to achieve spectacular results.

The World Wars: Tipping Points

Both the world wars threw up a number of technologies, innovations and weapons that affected the course of the wars. For example, telecommunications, submarines and electronic warfare changed the way military operations were conducted. The winners were those who could effectively integrate these inventions and concepts into their operational plans and make the best of them. Good leadership on the battlefield is all about understanding the potential of new technologies and weapon systems that can virtually enhance your force potential.

Tank Warfare

With the advent of tanks, the military commanders could devise new strategies and tactics to hit the enemy, especially during the First World War.

Within a decade and before the Second World War, the performance of tanks enhanced significantly and they became a decisive factor in any battle. The Allied and the Axis forces used artillery and air power in conjunction with infantry, thereby making this monster one of the first force multipliers of modern warfare.

General Heinz Guderian of the German army was the first to realize the potential of radio communication in tank warfare. He was convinced that a tank force with effective radio communication would have a tremendous advantage over the adversary. He demonstrated a field firing and depicted a battlefield scenario to Hitler to buy him in. Hitler immediately grasped the capability of this potent combination and ordered radios to be built for all German tanks. This became another force multiplier.

During the initial few years of war, especially the run up to France in 1940, the Germans cleverly used a concentration of tanks and mechanized infantry backed by close air support to unleash a blitzkrieg. The operations were well strategized and fully coordinated within the entire command and control hierarchy. They could thus deliver a massive blow to the enemy wherever they chose to hit. This is another example of force multiplication. It is a coordinated effort to synchronize the entire war machinery resulting in maximum impact.

Enigma and Deception

The Germans also came up with an encrypting machine, which could quickly convert a plain text message into an encrypted one that was almost impossible to break. This machine was nicknamed the 'Enigma'. In his book *The Ultra*

Secret, F.W. Winterbotham, an air force officer of the Royal Air Force, describes how the British managed to get hold of a few machines just before the start of the war without the knowledge of the Germans and put thousands of mathematicians, chess champions and linguists to work, who successfully decoded more than 10,000 German operational messages a day.

The Germans thought that their code could never be broken, but the British, with the help of these machines that were captured intact, managed to fool them throughout the war. Thus, the Enigma, which was supposed to be a game changer for the Germans, became a force multiplier for the British and the Allies. During a major period of the war, the intentions of the German high command, and their strategies and operational details were available to the British almost in real time. It was so critical to the Allied forces that they termed this operation 'Ultra Secret,' which is even beyond the 'top secret' classification and this shortened the war by several years. Winston Churchill, who was the direct beneficiary of this golden egg, said about the staff that decoded the messages day and night: 'The geese that laid the golden eggs and never cackled.' After the war, he told King George VI, 'It was thanks to Ultra that we won the war.'

Air Power

Tactical air reconnaissance gave 'long-range eyes' to the fighting forces. Aircrafts were used to get information regarding enemy locations, movements, logistics, critical areas and even terrain and weather. This was developed and used extensively by the Allies and the Axis forces. Air photo interpretation capability gave impetus to this concept. The side that used it effectively gained a considerable advantage in the war. The innovative use of aircraft changed the rules of the game during the Second World War.

With air power becoming a major force to reckon with, radars came up on the scene very quickly. Thousands of aircraft were used by both Allied and Axis forces and radars were deployed in large numbers by both sides. During the six-year conflict, this revolutionary technology greatly influenced the air defence capabilities of all the major nations that participated.

Almost at the end of the war, when the German armies were losing heavily, Hitler needed a wonder weapon to maintain the morale of his people. By the middle of 1944, German scientists had successfully created a 'vengeance weapon' known as the V-2 rocket. It was a single-stage short-range ballistic missile carrying a 1000-kg warhead. It could be launched from a mobile platform and had a range of 320 km. The Allies, including the Americans, did not have this weapon in their inventory. Hitler wanted to strike with full force at the United Kingdom (UK), mainly to demoralize the British. Therefore, in September 1944, more than 3,000 V-2 rockets were launched, mostly targeting London and Antwerp. Though the damage was not in proportion to the effort, it did dent the morale of the Allied forces in a big way.

Electronic Warfare

The invention of radio or wireless communication was something that gave military commanders an instant access to their resources. Field commanders could give orders, take feedback, observe, orient and take decisions with larger flexibility, which was not available to them earlier. Radio links and other means of communications had become commanders' lifeline and they were totally blinded without them.

Disrupting the enemy line of communication, therefore, was another breakthrough technology that emerged as a game changer. Since radio provided flexibility in mobile warfare, it was the first to be targeted for disruption. Radio jammers quickly came into the scene to play havoc with the radio communication of the adversary, and this could seriously handicap the effectiveness of any powerful military formation.

To counter these military planners, researchers came up with anti-jamming procedures and processes. Soon, technologies also sprung up to take measures against enemy jamming. Electronic countermeasures thus evolved as part of electronic warfare, which was soon recognized as a force to reckon with.

Terrain and Weather

On several occasions, especially during the Second World War, military commanders exploited weather situations and terrain to their advantage. Russians used their winters, rains and vast land cleverly to inflict heavy causalities on German armies. During the Second World War, the scorched-earth policy was an out-of-the-box solution by an almost defeated Russian Army. It was a strategic decision taken to destroy everything useful, while withdrawing from any area, so that the Germans could not make use of it. Therefore, retreating Russian forces destroyed oil dumps, communications, food and even buildings and shelters. Due to this, the German force, which was short of supplies, food and medicine, withered away in the cold Russian weather. The Russian cold and vast wasteland did more damage to the advancing German troops than any bombing.

Exploiting weather conditions during warfare is an

important part of a winning strategy. Nearly 2,500 years ago, Sun Tzu had said, 'Know yourself, your enemy; your victory will never be endangered. Know the ground, know the weather, your victory will then be total.' Almost at the fag end of the Second World War in 1944, the Allied forces were to cross the English Channel and attack the Germans entrenched on the French side. This was one of the largest operations of the war and was codenamed 'Operation Overlord'. A lot depended on the weather, because this operation involved thousands of ships carrying a very large number of troops, ammunition, tanks and several other pieces of military hardware across the English Channel over a very short period. General Eisenhower, the supreme Allied commander of Europe, had selected 5 June as the date of the assault. Unfortunately, on 4 June, the weather packed up, with high winds making landings unsuitable and low clouds not permitting air attacks. The Germans were pretty sure that in such weather conditions, the Allies would not be able to launch an invasion. So much so, that their top rung officers went on leave, which included field Marshal Rommel, who went home to attend his wife's birthday. On 5 June, Eisenhower was informed by the meteorological department that there would be slight improvement in the weather the next day. At a crucial meeting, taking into account all military aspects, Eisenhower decided to surprise the enemy by launching the invasion on 6 June itself. After a fierce battle on the beaches of Normandy for close to two months, the Allied forces eventually dislodged the Germans successfully. During the entire six years of war, many such tipping points occurred, mostly created by technology and a few by the exploitation of nature.

Several new technologies came into existence due to the long-drawn world wars. Post the Second World War, there was rapid progress in the field of electronics and telecommunications. Around the 1970s, computers came into the scene. This was the beginning of the Information Age. At the same time, the lethality and index of weapons also improved tremendously. Weapons became more precise and the speed of aircraft, ships, submarines and tanks increased manyfold. This, in turn, increased the speed of battles, conflicts became shorter and resolved faster and the reaction time available to a military commander shrunk considerably.

Controlling the Battle and Managing the Available Resources

During the Korean War (1950-1953), Colonel John Boyd of the US air force developed a concept for decision-making that came to be known as the OODA loop. As per this concept, decision-making is done in a cycle of 'Observe—Orient—Decide—Act'. First, you observe and collect information, then during orientation you analyse and synthesize the information, decide and thereafter, act according to the decision. Any force engaged in a conflict, who can process this cycle faster than the other(s), would gain a considerable advantage. This later became the basis for the command and control of a battlefield scenario.

The OODA loop shrunk over the centuries. During battles fought on horseback, it would take days, maybe months, to gather information, then more days to orient and decide, and still further to act. Today, information can be collected in real time. Orientation now takes very little time due to computer technology. In a matter of hours, decisions can be taken with the support of software, and action can take place immediately thereafter. As an example, Operation Desert Storm was a 100-hour war employing 125,000 aircraft sorties. It was a one-sided victory for the US through weapon-guiding systems, the communication satellite Satcom and electronic warfare. A short and intense war creates huge stress for the military leaders due to compressed reaction time and a very large force level to be deployed and redeployed quickly.

Therefore, today's force multipliers are highly technology intensive, and they all contribute to compress the OODA loop. The bottleneck in an OODA loop is at the 'orient' and 'decide' points. Orientation is like absorbing, interpreting and making sense of the observations to align one's thinking to the current scenario in real time. Interpretation is based on one's previous knowledge, experiences or even information available in earlier archived databases. Orientation is yet not totally automated and there is a fair amount of human element involved in this. The OODA loop was described for a single point of orientation and decision-making, which is far from real-life circumstances. Both in a war room and a corporate boardroom, there are a number of people who matter in the decision-making process. In other words, orientation is team work. This, therefore, becomes a bottleneck and delays the 'D', or decision. So, lack of decisions and more flow of information swamp the loop, and again, the OODA loop gets short-circuited from O to D. The very purpose of closing the loop quicker than the opponent is therefore defeated.

People who try to make sense of a situation use their previous experiences and their implicit knowledge. Each person has some implicit knowledge and interprets the data points against this knowledge. That is why the interpretations differ within a team. The way out is to push each person to convert the implicit knowledge into an explicit form by sharing it with others.

At the 'D' point or the decision-making stage, the most difficult part is to manage uncertainty. Orientation must work in sync with decision-making to come up with options or alternative plans. This helps the decision-maker, who tries to then control whatever he can and minimize the damage caused by what he cannot.

Modern Battlefield Information Systems

Electronic warfare (EW) soon became a new dimension of war. The EW spectrum had to be dominated and exploited. Apart from jamming the enemy's electronic-based systems, EW was extensively used for monitoring enemy communication and also get to know his intentions. Collecting and analysing signals and electronic radiations from radars, guidance systems and other military platforms also became a part of intelligence gathering. This is known as electronic support measures, which act as electronic eyes for a military commander.

Alongside this came the battlefield surveillance system, having an array of sensors to monitor the frontage for enemy activity and movement. Air defence systems evolved to manage and control air space. Artillery became a major weapon system and to control the power of hundreds of guns on a battle frontage, a highly sophisticated fire control system called 'artillery combat command and control system' was developed.

To integrate these key war-making components, a composite C4I (command, control, communication, computers and intelligence) system was created. At the heart of this is the command and information decision support system (CIDSS). All the other systems, like EW, the artillery combat command and control system, air defence system and battlefield surveillance system came together to make it one composite battlefield information system. In essence, such a system will help shrink the OODA loop.

This became the real force multiplier for modern armies. At the same time, telecom technology progressed very quickly. Transmitting and receiving hundreds of gigabytes per second became a reality. In fact, there was information overload. Had it not been for the CIDSS, a field commander would have been drowned by the information made available to him in real time.

As telecom technology improved, communication grid systems evolved, whereby formations could criss-cross across the battle zone, hooking and unhooking from the communication nodes in a defined geographical area. This development provided constant connectivity on the move. This is akin to the cellular technology now used extensively for urban mobile communication where a mobile subscriber moves in a grid consisting base transreceiver stations.

Across history, we constantly moved from brute forces to smart forces, largely due to a constant upgradation of weapon systems and decision support systems, with technology playing a pivotal role. A typical C4I system could be so designed as to handle a minimum force of 600 tanks, 400 combat vehicles, 400–450 heavy guns, 20,000–25,000 vehicles, 100–200 missile launchers, and more than 100,000 rifles and machine guns. Therefore, technology and smart force restructuring according to the available technology brought the biggest revolution in military affairs. Many modern armies are transforming their strategies, organizations, training and operations in an integrated manner to achieve spectacular results.

Technologies that Augmented Lethality, Index and Firepower

Stealth Technology

During the Second World War, radars came up in a big way and were to form the backbone of air defence systems. To avoid radar detection, the aircraft had to fly very low, almost at the height of treetops. This was not always possible and exposed the low-flying aircraft to threats from the ground as it could be easily shot down by the enemy.

Hence, 'low observable' technology or stealth technology was developed to make aircraft *almost* invisible to radars. It was like camouflaging it electromagnetically by reducing the radar cross section. Stealth technology is a combination of several methods and technologies such as non-metallic air frame, use of radar-absorbing materials and manipulating the shape and angles of the aircraft's body. Today, a stealth bomber cannot be detected by radars, allowing entry into enemy airspace and achieving maximum surprise.

Precision-Guided Ammunition

Accuracy of aim is one of the five most important features of a weapon system. Therefore, the quest for a precision weapon has been there since the beginning of human conflict. Precision weapons started emerging during the Second World War, but real equipment was invented much later during the Korean, Vietnam and Gulf wars. Precision-guided ammunition, as it is now called, is one of the most important developments of the 20th century.

Precision weapons depend on either their own guiding system or an external guiding system to direct a warhead against a single target, and can be controlled using radio, satellite or laser technology. Before these guided weapons were invented, precision depended on the soldier's aim alone. Now it largely relies on technology and that was the quantum shift. With such precision, one could destroy the target alone and cause no other collateral damage.

Global Positioning System

The race for space domination started immediately after the Second World War and the USSR and the US became the forerunners. Rocket science and intercontinental ballistic missiles, coupled with nuclear warheads, became the potential methods of mass destruction. However, as a nuclear war would annihilate both superpowers, these technologies thankfully were never used.

One of the most potent uses of space-based satellite technology is the global positioning system (GPS), which uses several satellites to provide location and time information anywhere on the earth in all weather conditions. A US initiative, it is now available to anyone with a GPS receiver. Initially meant for the military alone, in 1996 it was declared as a dual-use system and was allowed for civilian use as well. This technology has been a game changer for the human race.

Unquantifiable, Soft Force Multipliers

Morale

In simple words, morale is a state of mind. A demoralized army can never fight and can never win a war. Therefore, morale is one of the key factors that every force commander must keep in mind. In the armed forces, it is the duty of every officer to ensure that the morale of his troops is always high. A soldier takes pride in his being a soldier who is fighting for a higher cause. He takes pride in his unit, his uniform and being a comrade-at-arms. All these put together, keep a soldier going and keep his morale high, even while facing difficult times. A demoralized force of 1,000 men can be defeated by 100 highly charged and motivated men. This is the most intangible force multiplier. In civil parlance, the company you work for, your group dynamics and what kind of leader you work under determine your morale.

Discipline

Needless to say, a disciplined force can do wonders. Armies that have disciplined men and officers have always excelled. This is well documented in the history of warfare. An undisciplined force, however large, can never face a disciplined adversary.

Responsiveness

An armed contingent must respond to commands in the shortest possible time. Responsiveness refers to 'the ability to react quickly.' In a battlefield scenario, not only do the reflexes of individual soldiers matter, but the reflexes of a unit as a whole must also be faster than that of the adversary. Training people to act collectively is the biggest asset of the armed forces. Right up to the top of the pyramid, the system must respond quickly to every situation, demand or command. Armies who build responsiveness as a matter of habit have that edge over others. In the OODA loop, it is 'A' for action that finally delivers the punch.

Military commanders have always been in search of force multipliers in order to augment the capability of the team that is placed under their command. A field commander will always be short of manpower and weapons but his ingenuity lies in the ability to spot the existing force multipliers and being able to create new ones.

Revolution in Corporate Affairs

The business of managing warfare is very similar to managing corporate business, though in a battlefield, military commanders get lesser reaction time and a very large number of variables to play with. In the last two decades, technology has changed the way business is done and with whom it is done. It has also thrown up thousands of new business models and avenues that hitherto did not even exist. Today, if someone asks, 'What business can I do?', the number of ideas that will be thrown at him will probably swamp him.

In almost the same time frame, the world's political environment has also changed. From a bipolar world order where only the USSR and the US were the two forces to reckon with, it became unipolar with the disintegration of the former into many nation states. This quickly changed to a multipolar world order. The US is no more the only superpower, as other nations have also made enough progress to challenge it, not only economically but also militarily.

At the same time, the world business order has also transformed. There were more bilateral and regional cooperation initiatives undertaken and at the same time, many initiatives were conducted on worldwide platforms politically. Thus began the era of global cooperation, popularly known as 'globalization.' This was possible because of semiconductor technology, which brought in a revolution in communications and computing. Telecommunication technology took on a new avatar, majorly because of satellites, optical fiber, electronic switching, cellular technology and routers. At the same time, computers became faster, smarter, smaller and their memory capacities rose exponentially. From kilobytes per second in the 80s, we now use gigabytes per second and terabytes of data storage. The Internet is probably the biggest fusion of cutting edge technologies since the beginning of our history. And this was the biggest game changer of all times, especially for businesses. The World Wide Web has connected people in real time. Anyone who can plug into the Internet can access an unimaginably large amount of information and get across to all those connected likewise, anywhere in the world.

Soon, cellular technology connected everyone to the telephone network and eventually to the Internet via simple applications. At the time of writing this, for a world population of 7 billion, there are 6.8 billion cellphones! Theoretically, almost every human being will have a cellphone in the near future. On the back of this existing worldwide network emerged social media. Facebook and LinkedIn became the new force multipliers; in corporate parlance, these are also known as 'killer apps'. Suddenly, dominating the cyberspace was the top priority for each individual who worked for a living.

If the focus in the 80s was on process or business re-engineering, it is now on speed, though I would prefer to call it velocity in the present-day context. While velocity has an element of direction, speed is a scalar quantity. Multiple connectivity allows you to move with the speed of your thought in specific, chosen directions in and around a '360^0 opportunity continuum', changing directions at will.

New business models have now emerged and e-business and e-commerce have become a reality. Online is the new mantra, as you can buy most things online with the click of a mouse. With this kind of connectivity, your imagination is the only limitation to a new business avenue.

BOODA: The Business OODA Loop Has Shrunk

Before the advent of the Internet and its full penetration into business transactions, business-related communication depended on postal and telex networks and landline phones. Although the Transmission Control Protocol/Internet Protocol (TCP/IP) suite was finalized in 1982, it was conceived as the Internet much later in 1995, with just 1 per cent of the information flow as compared to today. Within five years, by the year 2000, it was handling 51 per cent, and by the year 2007, 97 per cent.[8]

The business of doing business has now changed. Much like modern warfare, new technologies are providing new ways of doing business and are severely influencing 'business doctrines'. Business is happening at the speed of thought and the reaction time for managers and senior business leaders has shrunk, which is indirectly creating 'business fatigue'.

Every day, there are new opportunities, challenges and competition. Innovative business decisions, government policies and new legislations can become force multipliers if business leaders remain alert. For instance in the US, California's ambitious Solar Program, with a target capacity of 3 Gigawatts by 2016, expected a million solar rooftops. Legislated by the government, it was an opportunity of sorts. It generated 25,000 jobs across 3,500 solar-based companies.

---

[8]Lumen Learning. The Internet. Retrieved from https://courses.lumenlearning.com/computerapps/chapter/reading-the-internet/

Most business boardrooms probably 'observed', but many neither could 'orient' nor 'decide' on a plan. They got bogged down with 'O—D'. Those business leaders who were able to exploit the political environment were very much like military leaders who exploited the weather to their advantage, while planning an invasion.

Technology leaders like chief information officers and chief technology officers must realize that a revolution in military affairs was not necessarily due to radical changes in military hardware. Armies used the same hardware, but augmented their effectiveness by putting together information-gathering systems and processing systems enabling the leadership to handle the shrunk OODA loop.

Therefore, learning from this, business enterprises need to use networking technologies, business intelligence, big data and enterprise application integration. Business analytics is an amalgamation of technologies, tools and methods for the continuous monitoring and analysis of past business trends and performances to give relevant inputs for business planning. It is highly scientific and evaluates business performance basis, data, statistical models, quantitative analysis and predictive modeling, which helps in decision-making, and closely resembles the CIDSS in a battlefield information system.

The move from business intelligence to business analysis has been similar to what happened in warfare strategies. Business intelligence, like military intelligence, was good enough to answer questions like 'What happened? How much force is available? Where is the bottleneck?' But business analytics is more to do with predictions and reasoning to answer questions like 'What if this scenario continues? Why is this happening? What would happen, say, a week later or a month later?' There is a component of embedded intelligence that needs to go into this. CIDSS systems are trying to utilize artificial intelligence to make their results more potent, but as of now, these systems are in the nascent stage of development.

Integrating Business Functions and Recent Trends in the Search of Game Changers

Business managers who integrate different segments like technology, manpower, environment, innovations and functions will do far better than those who don't. This is much like stitching together battlefield systems to make a seamless system that can respond to situations in real time. Several standalone inventions and products qualify to be viewed as game changers and act like force multipliers in a given context:

Integrated Business Strategy

For any business, customer satisfaction and aspirations are the most important. In order to ensure that they use customer inputs into their business strategy for overall success, business leaders must bring their sales, marketing, branding and product development teams together on the same page. Marketing must be a conduit between the product and sales teams, and marketing decisions cannot be taken in isolation without considering ground realities. Today, companies are even considering the human resource department as a strategic partner because a large amount is spent on acquiring quality workforce and results depend considerably on people's performance.

Enterprise Resource Planning (ERP)

ERP is a business management software that has several components that a company can use to collect, store, distribute, manage, analyse and interpret data from many business activities, like product planning, manufacturing or service delivery, marketing, sales and inventory management. It integrates business processes to project and provide a holistic view to the decision-makers as well all stakeholders in the organization. This increases the efficiency of an organization manyfold, as it tracks critical business resources like raw material, inventory, stocks, cash flow, production capacity and commitments like orders, deliveries and payouts almost in real time.

The major advantage of ERP is that it integrates multiple business processes and allows the management to take faster decisions at different levels, and with fewer errors. It makes data visible across the organization and is an organizational force multiplier.

Electronic Knowledge

The publishing industry is going through a big change, functionally and technologically. Today, a good publishing house gets the authors, editorial, creative, branding, sales and marketing people together. With fierce competition in book trade, the price points, discounts, cover design, title and packaging are all very important. Which cover design will stand out on the shelf where hundreds of other books are available cannot be decided by the author and the editorial department alone; the marketing team can often give very valuable inputs.

Technology has changed the publishing industry completely. Handling text and artwork have become simpler, thanks to the phenomenal word processing capabilities available on a computer. Co-authors can simultaneously work on a book, sitting in two different continents. Editors and authors can exchange content in near real time and make changes right up to the day the book goes to the press. E-books have become a reality and they create an avalanche of books on various reading platforms. E-book revenue is between 20–25 per cent of the total book sales in the Western world. The sales of printed books have dropped and many large bookshops have shut down because of stiff competition from online portals that provide heavy discounts, which they can afford as they have no inventory or infrastructure overheads.

Audio books are expected to be the next boom in this industry.

Handling Business Bottlenecks: A Paradigm Shift

Every business has a few bottlenecks that impede an enterprise. If these bottlenecks can be identified and removed, the system would become very efficient. In 1984, Eliyahu M. Goldratt, in his book *The Goal*, put forth a management paradigm that looks at a management system as being held back in achieving its goals by a very small number of constraints. This was popularly known as the 'Theory of Constraints'. There is always at least one constraint and this theory focuses on identifying that and restructuring the rest of the organization around it to get spectacular results.

In a nutshell, it follows the age-old idiom, 'A chain is as strong as its weakest link,' and identifies the weakest links that impede the progress of a process or an organization, ultimately finding ways and means to get rid of these bottlenecks, like people, processes, machinery and the like.

Theoretically, if there was nothing preventing a system from achieving higher output, its output would be infinite—which is impossible in a real-life system. Yet, this method can become a game changer for organizations, which can break their shackles of inefficiency by tweaking the right weak points. The process first identifies the constraints, then finds methods to eliminate them and finally and most importantly, subordinates everything else to the above decisions so that a change can be implemented. This last point is akin to the Germans using armoured divisions as the main force in their command and making all others, like infantry, artillery and air power, work in unison under the armour commander. The theory of constraints can be applied to a host of business verticals and functions like finance, sales, marketing, manufacturing, logistics and project management.

Education

Satellite communication and the Internet have changed the rules of the game for the education industry. Today webinars have replaced seminars and there are virtual classrooms. Teachers, while teaching a class of say 100 students, can teach thousands more anywhere in the world, who can listen to them, interact with them and learn through a simple video link. A sought-after professor need not fly to different locations, and can impart knowledge online.

Medicine

In the 19th century, surgery was often a desperate and last resort. Over the years, several techniques were used to dull the pain, like narcotics and even hypnotism. A direct way to induce a state of unconsciousness was to knock the patient off with a hard blow to the jaw. Opium and alcohol were tried, but with little success. Surgeons faced a major challenge and had to put up with yelling and screaming patients, which was a horrible experience for both doctor as well as patient.

General anesthesia has been a force multiplier in the medical industry. Doctors can now conduct major surgeries like open-heart surgery, orthopedic interventions and organ transplant, which would have been impossible otherwise.

Politics

The US presidential elections are an eye-opener for two reasons. One, that social media is a game changer; and two, that the game changers also change very quickly. In 2007, when Barack Obama announced his candidacy, Twitter had just started. Facebook and LinkedIn were also taking baby steps. By the time of the next elections in 2012, things had changed substantially. Not only had Internet penetration and the user base of Facebook gone up substantially, Twitter had also became pretty well populated.

In 2012, Obama had exploited social media to the hilt. It was not that he himself was tech-savvy, but he had a very forward-looking and innovative support team. He got double the likes on Facebook as compared to his adversary Romney. On Twitter, he got almost 20 times more retweets. He thus managed to create a new socio-political dialogue. For Obama, social media managers created a force multiplier.

In India, national political parties are up for a social media blitzkrieg, which each one would like to unleash on the other. They have realized the potential of this new force multiplier. With cell phone penetration in even rural areas, SMS campaigns can become a game changer. It allows parties to target the voter directly, select groups based on religion or region and send their message like a precision-guided ammunition. The days of banners, hoardings and posters may be over.

The Essence of Force Multiplication

The crux of force multiplication lies in the integration of processes, machines, people, power and technology. Therefore, five most important corporate silos for consideration are:

- Organizational structure
- Culture
- Manpower and training
- Technology and futuristic trends
- Leadership

Identifying Force Multipliers

It is important for business leaders to identity existing force multipliers. You have to keep asking, 'How can we make things better with the existing resources?' How do you make 3×3=9 instead of 3+3=6? Harnessing and adapting to new technologies and trends are the most important roles of business leaders today. They have to master the art of handling business intelligence. Assessing the political climate and the state of morale of your workforce is very important. Simple things like optimizing your website presence using search engine optimization can make a positive difference to your business. People have little time to spare and an opportunity missed is lost to your competitor. Appreciating the power and patency of an idea is the essence of modern-day leadership.

A decade back, I observed a guest lecture, where the lecturer asked the students, 'If you have a product that you want to promote and you have zero budget for advertisement, then how will you do it?' After struggling for almost 15 minutes, the class of 100 students could not give a satisfactory answer. The lecturer then answered his own question by showing a YouTube video that ran for just 1.39 minutes. It showed innovative ways to market a blender where a person takes a handful of diamonds (imitations of diamonds) and puts them in the blender to make a fine powder in seconds! This video had 6,394,822 hits at the time of writing. The key search word for this video is diamonds and it is one of the most searched words by women, who also use blenders in their kitchen! With this one simple idea, he could make his product reach out to more than 6 million people and, of course, the ones who would be interested in his product.

The world is in transition where change is the only constant. In such a scenario, business managers must always keep their ear to the ground to appreciate which technology will become obsolete at what point of time. Technology obsolescence can hit one's budgets very hard. When to upgrade and when not to, could be a million-dollar question at times.

Constantly watching and exploiting federal policies can also become a force multiplier.

Demanding a Force Multiplier

This is the most important lesson that needs to be learnt from the armed forces—they demand what they want. The concept of a general staff qualitative requirement is a practice followed by most armies. The user demands what he wants by specifying a qualitative requirement and the R&D team works on it. For instance, keeping modern warfare in mind, the artillery unit may demand a gun with a specific warhead to be delivered across a specific range; the air force may require a helicopter that needs to fly in the rarefied atmosphere of a high-altitude glacier, etc.

During the Second World War, Hitler demanded a

vengeance weapon to demoralize the Allies, especially Britain, and he got one. But he messed up on the development of an atomic bomb. The Germans did start working on it just before the war broke out months after the discovery of a nuclear fission in January 1939, but by the end of that year, when Germany attacked Poland, the German army's top brass ordered everyone to be drafted into the army, regardless of their qualifications or profession. Therefore, many notable physicists were enrolled to fight on the front! In 1933, many had fled Germany when Hitler assumed power because of his anti-Semitism stance. Hitler gradually politicized the education system and stressed more on Nazism than academic excellence. Some top scientists were also executed by the Nazis since they were Jews, and many top-notch physicists got drawn into research in mundane areas of defence demands.

In short, the Nazis under Hitler never appreciated the power of an atomic weapon and never looked at it as a game changer, whereas it actually was one. On the other hand, when Albert Einstein wrote a letter to US President Franklin D. Roosevelt, bringing to his notice that Germany was already working on an atomic weapon that could be a game changer, he immediately responded and Project Manhattan was commissioned to work on an atomic bomb. Between 1939–45, close to $2 billion had been spent and by mid-July 1945, the US tested its nuclear weapon. Two bombs were dropped on Nagasaki and Hiroshima on 6 and 9 August 1945 respectively, which changed the course of the war and brought it to a closure.

In the case of Germany, it was a colossal waste of talent they already had, while the Americans realized its worth and pushed the project with all their might.

Business leaders must learn two things out of this. First,

learn to define your own needs and requirements that will augment your work and help optimize operations. Second, make it into a qualitative requirement and then push the system to deliver it. If you want a new technology tool, then let the chief of technology create it or buy it. If it concerns process modernization, then let the top management come up with a solution.

Force Multiplier Consultants

Management consultants, in a way, help companies enhance their performance. They should start looking at force multipliers that already exist within the system and advise the management to use them effectively. In addition, they must bring in new technologies, processes and human resource development techniques to create new force multipliers for the organization. This can be a new consulting business where experts in consultation with the corporate clients can identify and propose an appropriate force multiplier for an existing business model.

In the armed forces, military commanders demand equipment to meet their technical, operational and tactical needs. They lay down in detail the technical and operational requirements of such weapon or support systems. However, business leaders only use new technologies that have emerged out of universities or commercial labs and use it to the best of their ability. They happen to remain satisfied with that. Very seldom does a company's top brass say, 'We want something with the following specifications; now let someone develop it.' Business leaders must demonstrate this hunger.

5

Economy of Effort and Concentration of Force

> *'Act with utmost concentration and act with the utmost speed.'*
>
> —General Von Clausewitz

Force and Resource Management

Economy of effort, concentration of force and having a reserve or a backup for unforeseen eventualities are all interrelated areas, which are collectively termed 'force and resource management'. In the context of a battle, it is important to appreciate that for a force to be effective, it needs adequate weapons and equipment. On the other hand, without an adequate fighting force, no amount of weapons and equipment can result in a victory. Therefore, economy of effort and concentration of force need to cater in equal measures to both the manpower as well as the equipment required for a military operation. Economy of effort and maintaining a reserve should be viewed more as an attitude rather than a principle. Not having an 'inbuilt' reserve is unthinkable for any field commander and is as good as committing a sin.

Concentration of Force

Concentration of force is one principle of war that has held its ground since the dawn of warfare. Sun Tzu, in his classic work *The Art of War*, written almost 2,500 years ago, put forth some classic 'fundamentals of fighting'. Concentration of force is one such fundamental principle strongly recommended by him: 'We can form a single united body while the enemy must split up into fractions, hence there will be a whole pitted against separate parts of a whole, which means that we shall be many to the enemy's few. And if we are able to thus attack an inferior force with a superior one, our opponent will be in dire straits.'

He also says that the 'enemy, like ourselves, has limited resources and hence, if he strengthens his front, he will weaken his rear; should he strengthen his rear, he will weaken his front; if he strengthens his left; he will have a weak right and vice versa.'

General Carl Von Clausewitz had said, 'Pursue one great decisive aim with force and determination.' He made force concentration an integral part of the Prussian military doctrine called 'mass decision', or 'mass at decisive point', which was aimed at causing disproportionate losses on the enemy, destroying his ability to fight. It was like hitting someone with a sledge hammer. He was of the opinion that since it was difficult to have a very high numerical superiority over the enemy, concentration of force was imperative for a decisive victory. He was to influence military strategy and tactics for the next century and his ideas are still respected by the military fraternity.

During the Second World War, military commanders got an opportunity to undertake larger roles and this principle got fully embedded into the military doctrines of most modern armies. A military commander will always be running short of resources, men as well as material. The single biggest problem facing anybody who is fighting a war is 'scarcity'. The art of optimizing and making the best use of resources is the key to success. Therefore, no part of manpower and resources should be left without purpose and when the time comes for execution, all resources should have a task to perform.

Looking at it scientifically,

$$\text{Pressure} = \text{Force applied} \div \text{Area}$$

This translates into force per unit area. To illustrate its effect, let us look at a knife that has a sharp blade and another that has a blunt one. The sharp blade implies lesser surface area and hence it's able to cut through an object more easily by applying a moderate force as compared to the blunt one, which has a much larger surface area. Similarly, a sharp arrow can easily pierce through a surface compared to a blunt one.

In a military scenario, if there are four units available to the defender as well as the attacker, there can be different ways of using these combat units. If the defender has to hold a long defensive line, then he sequentially deploys all four units next to each other along that line. Therefore, each segment of the defending line is held by a single unit. It is generally accepted that the defender has an advantage of 3:1. Therefore, only if the attacker uses three out of four units, can he make a dent in the enemy defence.

Therefore, for the attacker it makes more sense to employ three units against one, on a shorter frontage (a single point) rather than employing them on a large frontage area. Concentration of force requires mobilizing and coordination. The advantage of the attacker is that he can choose where and when to attack. The defender also needs to have at least one unit that can be quickly moved to the place of attack so that the attacker loses the 3:1 advantage.

Economy of Force

When Winston Churchill was asked the secret of his success, he said, 'Economy of effort. Never stand up when you can sit down, never sit down when you can lie down.'[9] On the battlefield, every man and every round counts. One cannot afford to waste even the most insignificant resource.

At the planning stage, it is important to define the roles and responsibilities of each group and fighting unit. The role is the broader aspect that defines where that unit fits into the entire plan of action. For example, the role of a unit could be to protect the flank of a larger formation. On the other hand, the responsibilities will be detailed instructions for actions when the battle starts.

Many times in the heat of battle, force commanders plan for an overkill. It is like flogging a dead horse, and goes against the principle of economy of force and effort. Murphy's Law of Combat says that, generally speaking, the best tank killer is another tank. Using a tank to destroy a tank is a waste of precious resource. One can also use a rocket launcher or throw a grenade down the open hatch of a tank to destroy a tank. Never use cannon to kill a crow! In a nutshell, it means the judicious use of resources. Great generals were known to use the right amount of force at the right time at the right place. They made sure that their forces complemented each other so that the whole was greater than the sum of the parts.

---

[9]Foreman, J. (2009). Winston Churchill, Distilled. Retrieved from https://winstonchurchill.org/resources/in-the-media/churchill-in-the-news/winston-churchill-distilled/

In kung fu or any classic martial art, there is a principle of 'minimum effort and maximum impact'. In judo, for instance, one can use the strength of a charging opponent to execute a throw. You act like a pivot and use his kinetic energy to throw him over your shoulder. Good boxers save their breath; they also exhaust the opponent by letting them spend their energy first. Once they are tired, only then do they go for the kill.

To obtain victory in any battle, one should be like water and adapt to the situation. Water always finds the path of least resistance. Learn to speed up or slow down and expand or contract depending on the situation. Water also takes the shape of the vessel in which it is stored. In a cup, it takes the shape of the cup, and in a bottle, it takes the shape of the bottle. That is the way to use your force as well as energy.

Skippers of good cricket teams conserve their best batsmen and bowlers and get them into the field at the right time and in front of the right player of the opposing team.

Economy of force is a life skill and attitude that must be constantly applied till it becomes a habit.

Tactics and Strategies for Maximum Effect: Concentration of Force

Force concentration and economy have been a part of military commanders' repertoire since the advent of warfare. Keeping the principle of optimal utilization of resources as well as managing to deliver a decisive blow to the enemy resulted in different tactical and strategic applications on the battlefield. Some of the prominent ones are discussed below:

Rapid Dominance: Shock and Awe

This can be used as a strategic initiative by an attacking

force that has an overwhelming superiority over the enemy, not only in numbers, but also with technology, firepower, intelligence, coordination and rapidity. It aims at affecting the morale, perception and even the ability to judge the quantum of force being brought in by the attacking force, and renders the enemy incapable of responding and hitting back. It paralyses the military as well as the political decision-making system of the defending forces. In short, it stuns the enemy. In recent times, Americans have used this during the Iraq War, which began with a massive, simultaneous air strike across all major cities of Iraq including Baghdad. It demoralized the Iraqi army and caused confusion at the military commander's level. The idea of rapid dominance is to minimize the casualties of one's troops and quickly end the war. While the former is achievable because of superior technology and surprise, the latter would depend on several other factors like the terrain, depth and spread of enemy forces.

Nuclear Attack

The atomic bombing of Nagasaki and Hiroshima at the end of the Second World War was undertaken by the Allied forces to end the war quickly by making the Japanese surrender. The impact of these two bombs was such that the Japanese military and their government, which was initially adamant about not surrendering, had no choice but to do the same unconditionally.

Air Force

The use of aircraft in combat became predominant in the Second World War, though it had demonstrated its potency during the First World War in a limited way. Massive air raids dominated the six-year-long Second World War and a notion of 'air supremacy' was part of any military operation at the strategic as well as tactical level. Air forces had massive destructive power with their bombing and staffing capabilities and had the necessary speed to act quickly. Close air support at the tactical level was often a game changer for ground forces engaged in combat with the enemy on the front. At a strategic level, a well-planned bomber raid involving a large number of aircraft was enough to pulverize a city and demoralize any army or ground force.

Tank Warfare

Shock and awe was yet again witnessed when the battle tank became a part of the military arsenal. Like aircraft, it had a limited role in the First World War, which was dominated by trench warfare. The Germans were the first to employ radio communication in tanks, thus improving the command and control of a mobile force manyfold. With this came the shock and awe tactics popularly known as blitzkrieg. The philosophy underlying the blitzkrieg was to use a concentration of force, almost like a knife piercing straight and deep into the enemy's heart. Massive tank force backed by infantry and artillery was applied on a very short frontage to make a dent. Thereafter, one's forces galloped rapidly into the enemy territory.

Human Wave

In 1962, the Indo-China War was a demonstration of numerical superiority by the Chinese army. It used human wave tactics with a numerical superiority of more than 5:1 and most of the Indian posts on the border were drowned by the massive Chinese forces that attacked from several directions simultaneously. The Chinese were also prepared to use their human resources as cannon fodder and therefore relied more on numerical superiority rather than better technology or weapons.

Carpet Bombing

As the name suggests, carpet bombing is done over a selected area, where every part of the said area is pelted by serial bombing. The damage completely covers the area in a way a carpet would cover a floor. This could be done by artillery fire or by using aircraft. This is a 'brute force' technique and does not use precision bombing, which destroys select targets only. Special weapon systems like multi-barrel rocket launchers, which can fire more than a dozen rockets each, while carrying hundreds of kilograms of payload in less than a minute, are now in the possession of modern armies. These can completely destroy an area as big as 4–5 km^2 in a matter of minutes.

In artillery tactics, there is a concept of concentration of firepower, where a large number of guns simultaneously bring down heavy fire upon a target to inflict maximum damage. Napalm bombs were also used to create shock and fear in the enemy by Americans during the Vietnam War and earlier to some extent in the Second World War. They cause extensive damage to targets by inflicting severe burns to humans.

Barrage

When an enemy area needs to be captured, the main element of that force is the infantry, which goes and attacks the target, and later captures and holds the ground physically. In most cases, such a force goes on foot while attacking enemy posts.

To reduce the enemy's capability of bringing fire onto the advancing infantry on foot, there is a need to provide covering fire. Artillery fire is brought across an imaginary horizontal line in front of the advancing troops, which gives them adequate protection. The infantry thereafter moves behind the 'advancing barrage,' referred to as the creeping barrage, which is lifted and moved in small increments of usually a 100 yards every few minutes, keeping pace with the advancing infantry. This ensures that friendly troops do not get harmed due to their own fire. Since the barrage brings down sudden heavy firing on the enemy, this word has entered the general language where it has come to mean an intense sequence of apparently never-ending questions.

Terrorism

This is a form of asymmetric warfare where belligerents have significantly different war-waging capabilities. Therefore, the weaker group resorts to hitting at soft targets to get the desired results. Terrorist organizations need sensationalization so that the target group or nation gets the message. In addition, they get the desired publicity. A small group can create a deep impact by blowing up a vital resource or killing innocent people. Terror groups use deadly explosives against a soft civilian target to make a big impact. This is a classic example of economy of force. Guerrilla warfare may not use similar tactics, but operate much the same way as they also engage the soft spots of the enemy. Hit-and-run is a common tactic employed by them.

Each of the above methods gets a commander maximum bang for the buck.

Reserve Force

While following the principle of concentration of force to achieve maximum impact, the concept of reserve force cannot be overlooked. A general cannot commit all his resources to an operation without keeping something in his kitty to respond to any unexpected or unforeseen situation. One should therefore always remember Field Marshal Von Moltke's axiom that no battle plan survives contact with the enemy. Therefore, every sound military operation, tactical or strategic, always has a reserve built into the plan. The reserve force is more effective if it is mobile and can be quickly deployed anywhere in the entire area of responsibility.

During the Second World War, the Allied forces planned a massive operation across the English Channel to dislodge the Germans from France. Operation Overlord, planned by the Allies, was to see thousands of ships and a very large number of Allied forces cross the channel and land on the other side defended by the Germans. This was later popularly termed as 'Normandy Landings'. Field Marshal Rommel was in charge of the German defensive measures. He wanted the armoured formations to be deployed close to the coast to meet the enemy head-on and have a mobile reserve formation in a central place, to be placed under his command and mobilized and used appropriately as the battle unfolded.

Unfortunately, Hitler overruled his proposal, gave him only three Panzer divisions, and allowed only one to be kept close to the Normandy beaches, scattering others to be deployed along the entire coast. This was against the fundamental principle of concentration of force. As if this was not enough, the reserve force was kept under the German Armed Forces

Headquarters, which too was scattered across Belgium, France and the Netherlands. Not surprisingly, these were not made available to Rommel as and when he required. In the end, he could not offer adequate resistance to the British and American forces that landed on the Normandy beaches. As a result, the Allied forces were able to successfully make a bridgehead to launch an offensive, eventually liberating France.

Concept of a Bridgehead

Whenever an attacking force has to cross a water body or a large obstacle and has to then assault enemy defences, there is a need to bring a substantial force to first secure a foothold and then pierce a hole in the enemy defence. Since the enemy is well entrenched, he can rain heavy fire on the advancing troops, using both artillery fire and air power. Once a foothold is managed, the captured arc is expanded to form a secured bridgehead, which then becomes like a conduit through which a large force can cross over and enter the enemy area. This also serves as a lodgement area before breaking out into the enemy territory. Securing a bridgehead is an uphill task and unless the principle of concentration of force is applied, such an operation will result in massive casualties and often result in a failed operation.

The second half of 1942 was a critical period for the British and Allied forces in North Africa. The port of Alexandria was located 100 km east of El Alamein, which had the sea on one side and the impossible Qattara desert on the other, providing a narrow 60 km corridor. General Rommel of the German Army was pitted against General Harold Alexander and General Bernard Montgomery of the British army.

In order to access the port of Alexandria, the British forces had to penetrate through the 60 km corridor that was heavily mined by the Germans. In an overnight operation, 30 corps was assigned the task of making a breach and securing a bridgehead, so that two Allied armoured divisions could pass through.

Four infantry divisions with an overall strength of 80,000 men launched the main attack to create a corridor 10 km wide and 6 km deep. It was constructed through the enemy's defences. In addition to silencing the enemy, the assaulting troops had to clear the minefields and make the corridor safe, so that the two armoured divisions having 700 tanks could pass through and go for the kill, fortifications and tank formations. Through this corridor, almost 1,000 tanks and vehicles had to drive through in a matter of hours.

In business, if a company wants to expand to different territories, it is important to first secure a place as a lodging area, where the workforce and material can be positioned safely before launching a full-blown marketing campaign. This, in military operations, is also known as a firm base. Once a firm base is established, it becomes a safe haven whereupon finishing the daily chores, the teams can come and rest and replenish for the next day. Until and unless business is fully established and reasonable territory is captured, investment should not be made for a proper office or operating space.

Economy of Effort in Business

Business is all about economy of effort. The easier it is, the cheaper. The cheaper it is, the more profitable. If a job can be well planned and executed by five people, why do you need to hire eight to do it? Companies are operating on thin profit margins as competition is becoming stiffer. Therefore, economy of effort becomes an integral part of any business model. Management is nothing but common sense in most cases. For every business strategy, one must ask a simple question, 'Could it be done in an easier way, with lesser efforts and lesser resources?' Keep looking for an easier way till you hit a dead end, and that would be the best solution!

Simplicity is yet another important tenet of economy of effort. Keep your plans as simple as possible. Albert Einstein had said, 'If you can't explain it to a six-year-old, you don't understand it yourself.' Sometimes when I sit through some business presentations, I am amazed how B-school graduates try to complicate the simplest of things by throwing in jargons, making complex diagrams and quoting more facts than required. They unnecessarily add a lot of redundant stuff that complicates things rather than simplifying them.

In the early 1900s, workers in car factories assembled each vehicle kept on a specially designed rig. All the parts were brought to them by stock runners. This was a slow and costly process. The assembly line, a concept pioneered by Henry Ford, revolutionized the manufacturing industry. By 1913, he fully automated his plant where a partly assembled vehicle was moved on a conveyer belt and along the way, workers assembled one part at a time. This was later dubbed as 'work in motion'. Within a short span of time, his factory was rolling out one car every ten seconds. This could be the best example of economy of effort.

When businesses shifted from manufacturing to providing services, the focus shifted to processes. IT, IT-enabled services, hospitality, aviation and consulting started working on processes to reduce human intervention. Process-driven systems focus on streamlining businesses and are in line with economy of effort. To cater to aberrations and unforeseen requirements, these processes had inbuilt flexibility, so as to be able to react to such requirements by diverting efforts elsewhere, as and when required.

Concentration of Force in Business

Advertising and marketing are the two best contenders for using concentration of force as their basic principle. Unless you do aggressive marketing and aggressive advertising with a full force at your command, the results will always be dismal.

The founder of Crawford's Advertising Agency, one of the oldest and finest advertising agencies, Sir William Crawford spelt out the principles of advertising in three simple words: concentration, dominance and repetition. See how closely this resembles the military concepts of concentration of force, shock and awe, carpet bombing and rapid dominance!

During the First World Wars, British engineer Fredrick Lanchester formulated a law to calculate the combat effectiveness of military forces deployed against each other, which stated that the combat power of a unit force is the square of the number of members of that unit. Therefore, the larger unit will have the advantage, which will be the difference of the squares of the two forces. Therefore, if we consider two forces pitted against each other with five and three units or men, the larger force then has an advantage of $5^2 - 3^2 = 16$.

Though, there can be a number of business applications of this law, the most important aspect is the need for concentration of force. How can small defeat big? The answer lies in deploying your force in a smaller area, thus denying the enemy the advantage of a bigger force.

During the Napoleonic Wars, British Navy officer Lord Nelson's smaller fleet of ships was pitted against the combined fleet of France and Spain. He cleverly split the two fleets and concentrated his attack one at a time to eventually win without even losing one ship.

In the UK, Japanese photocopy machine manufacturer Canon used Lanchester's law to capture the market against their rival, Xerox. Canon first put all their might and sales force in Scotland and captured a sizeable market share in that region. Gradually, they moved on to selected and well-defined regions in the UK. Simultaneously, they invested in product improvement, keeping their workforce at the same level for a while. Gradually, they expanded their marketing team and then entered the bigger market—London. By then, they had a better product, a sizeable presence in the market across UK and a numerically superior marketing team. By this time, Xerox realized that they had already lost out to Canon.

6

Propaganda: Creating Virtual Reality

> *'If you tell a lie big enough and keep repeating it, it will become the truth, as people will eventually come to believe it.'*
>
> —Joseph Goebbels

What Is Propaganda?

One of the oldest pursuits of the human race has been to convince others and win support for their own viewpoint. For centuries, religious groups, preachers, members of cults or those with certain ideological beliefs, emperors and democratically elected politicians have tried to sell a point of view to their target audiences. Across history, they have all used propaganda to achieve this. People in power, including Napoleon, cleverly adopted innovative methods of communication to influence people. As propaganda, Alexander the Great installed his statues and used his image on coins to influence his subjects, armies as well as his opponents. Julius Caesar was exceptionally good at influencing his people and his enemies by applying propaganda. Martin Luther quickly realized the potential of the printing press and used it effectively in his fight against the Catholic Church. And America was lured into entering the First World War by convincing the American public and politicians that it was in the country's interest. In the 19th century, political cartoons became an effective way of propaganda.

These cartoons had potent use during the two world wars. Today, businesses employ various branding, advertising and marketing tools to influence buyers or to create product/service preferences over others.

In a broad sense, propaganda is a tool for mass motivation or mass mind management. Propaganda is supposed to act as an intermediary vehicle that'll dominate public opinion, address mass concerns and make the electorate cognizant of state policies, important events and viewpoints.

There are several definitions of 'propaganda'. Communications researcher Richard Alan Nelson gives a comprehensive and operational definition:[10]

> Propaganda is neutrally defined as a systematic form of purposeful persuasion that attempts to influence the emotions, attitudes, opinions and actions of specified target audiences for ideological, political or commercial purposes through the controlled transmission of one-sided messages (which may or may not be factual) via mass and direct media channels. A propaganda organization employs propagandists who engage in propagandism—the applied creation and distribution of such forms of persuasion.

Hype and propaganda are not too different from each other, because as per their definitions, both rely on exaggerated claims through publicity. Public relations, lobbying, branding and advertising are all different forms of propaganda and employ similar techniques to achieve their ultimate goal.

---

[10]McNearney, A. (2018). This WWII Cartoon Taught Soldiers How to Avoid Certain Death. Retrieved from https://www.history.com/news/wwii-propaganda-private-snafu-flashback

Psychological warfare is a form of propaganda employed at strategic, operational and tactical levels of the armed forces. It provides advantage to military commanders in their own areas of influence. Therefore, it has a much larger connotation than mere advertising, and has a direct impact not only on international relations, geodiplomacy and geopolitics, but it is equally potent for the propagation of religion, beliefs and ideologies that might be political or otherwise, in nature.

Propaganda is basically the propagation of faith or sowing the seeds of a particular thought. It has two models. The authoritarian model as used by the Germans, the Soviets and the Chinese, which employs coercion in support of persuasion; and the democratic model, which uses consensus, persuasion, minimal censorship and issue-based news.

Propaganda is broadly divided into many categories. It is white propaganda when the source is clearly known and there is no secrecy; grey propaganda, when the source appears to be ambiguous and not disclosed; and black propaganda, when it appears to have originated from the enemy. Such a form of propaganda is employed to embarrass or misrepresent the enemy.

In the last hundred years, communication technology has grown exponentially. This has given a different dimension to the effectiveness, speed and reach of propaganda as a technique. This was evident in the two world wars.

Propaganda during Wars

Propaganda during the First World War

Modern psychological warfare started during the First World War. At the beginning of the war, both the Germans and British were not organized enough to launch a proper propaganda campaign against each other. Nor did they realize the potential of propaganda. Several government departments handled British propaganda, as there was no central agency deputed to manage such an important issue. Germans also were in a similar situation. The British eventually did create a Ministry of Information in 1918—almost four years after the war started. Psychological warfare was therefore limited to dropping and distributing pamphlets on the front to demoralize the enemy. The British highlighted their humane treatment of German prisoners and talked ill about the German army's top brass. Millions of leaflets were distributed for the consumption of frontline German soldiers, describing them as mere 'cannon fodder' by German generals.

Domestically, both used similar mediums to reach out to their people to keep their morale high and seek more recruitment into the armed forces. To garner world opinion, the British had the distinct advantage of a very reliable and respected news network, which ran across the world. They also had good diplomatic corps, which could influence the leadership of nations that mattered to them. At that time, the British had several undersea cables that helped them to reach out to the world.

America played an important if not pivotal role in both the great wars. It was one of the biggest industrial nations when the First World War started. At some point during the war, the British realized that they could not make it alone and required America to enter. The American political leadership wanted to follow the policy of neutrality and therefore needed to be coaxed into taking the plunge. It was also important to build a positive American public opinion about the ongoing British war efforts against Germany, which in turn had to be projected in poor light. The British launched covert propaganda through news articles and books in order to reach out to opinion makers and decision drivers. They also utilized the services of some top actors, philosophers and intellectuals to influence those Americans who could influence American foreign policy.

The Germans also contributed in certain ways, forcing America to enter the war. Though US President Woodrow Wilson kept America away for more than two and a half years, the American public and opinion makers were heckled by repeated German submarine attacks on American commercial ships, forcing America to enter the war in April 1917.

Propaganda during the Second World War

Germany under the Nazis and Hitler

During the Second World War, under Hitler, propaganda acquired a negative connotation and pejorative meaning. Not surprisingly, the British and the Americans also used all their might to counter German propaganda and therefore, the term 'counter-propaganda' emerged.

Hitler had realized the power of manipulating people's minds much before embarking upon his political career. He devoted two chapters on propaganda in his book *Mein Kampf*, which, though written in 1925, became the central inspiration for the Nazi Party in later years. Hitler's charismatic oratory and effective propaganda skills added teeth to their well-thought-out strategy, where other components included emotional manipulation and rousing national sentiment. It was an altogether well-orchestrated plan, to make a nation dance to their tune!

Hitler understood the public 'sentimental phenomena' very early and therefore used emotional shockwaves to mobilize the Germans like never before. From his experience of the First World War, he knew where and how the British and other European nations had mobilized extensive propaganda against Germany. He had observed that during the First World War, the common citizens were horrified to see the use of new weapons like tanks, powerful bombs and automatic machine guns. These arms could brutally mass murder people and this terrorized the public. The Nazis under Hitler realized that modern warfare would require effective use of propaganda to sway public opinion. Not only was the military at war, an entire nation would get involved. Public opinion therefore had to be considered while deciding any policy. The morale of a nation would determine how civilians would sign up for military service and how much comfort they would be willing to sacrifice. Hitler's lessons in managing public perception were therefore, well-prepared.

Hitler had once said, 'Leaders are so lucky that people don't think.' In chapter VI of *Mein Kampf*, he wrote,

> Propaganda must always address itself to the broad masses of the people. All propaganda must be presented in a popular form and must fix its intellectual level so as not to be above the heads of the least intellectual of those to whom it is directed. The art of propaganda consists precisely in being able to awaken the imagination of the public through an appeal to their feelings, in finding the appropriate psychological form that will arrest the attention and appeal to the hearts of the national masses. The broad masses of the people are not made

up of diplomats or professors of public jurisprudence nor simply of persons who are able to form reasoned judgement in given cases, but a vacillating crowd of human children who are constantly wavering between one idea and another.

The great majority of a nation is so feminine in its character and outlook that its thought and conduct are ruled by sentiment rather than by sober reasoning. This sentiment, however, is not complex, but simple and consistent. It is not highly differentiated, but has only the negative and positive notions of love and hatred, right and wrong, truth and falsehood.

As for the methods to be employed, he went on to explain:

Propaganda must not investigate the truth objectively and, in so far as it is favorable to the other side, present it according to the theoretical rules of justice; yet it must present only that aspect of the truth which is favorable to its own side. The receptive powers of the masses are very restricted and their understanding is feeble. On the other hand, they quickly forget. Such being the case, effective propaganda must be confined to a few bare essentials and those must be expressed as far as possible in stereotyped formulas. These slogans should be persistently repeated until the very last individual has come to grasp the idea that has been put forward. Every change that is made in the subject of a propagandist message must always emphasize the same conclusion. The leading slogan must of course be illustrated in many ways and from several angles, but in the end one must always return to the assertion of the same formula.

Hitler's Nazi Party came to power by whipping up German emotions and continued with its propaganda and manipulation from 1925 to 1933, when Hitler became the chancellor of Germany. After coming to power, he wanted to employ an aggressive propaganda strategy and created the Reich Ministry of Public Enlightenment and Propaganda, appointing a close confidante and former journalist, Dr Joseph Goebbels, its minister. Within a few years, Goebbels organized the ministry from a mere concept a full-blown, mind-manipulating machine. They needed a few strong symbols, or hate points, and found these in Jews and the Treaty of Versailles.

The latter was projected as the external enemy, designed to destroy the German state. The treaty was signed under protest and Chancellor Frederick Schliemann had remarked, 'May the hand that signs this treaty wither.' Schliemann had even resigned from office, refusing to take the onus on himself. Since every German hated the treaty, Hitler and his cronies wanted to use this fact to their complete advantage. Jews were the internal enemies of the state. Hitler's philosophy against the Jews was that they had inflicted two great wounds on humanity—circumcision of the body and the conscience of the soul.

At the beginning of the war, German propaganda was for internal consumption and aimed at manipulating every German mind. Germans staying in France, Poland, Belgium and the USSR were repeatedly told that they were being discriminated against and put to misery by the local governments. This made Germans staying abroad go against their governments. Besides, it generated a sympathy wave for the Nazi Party as expat Germans urged their kith and kin in Germany to applaud Hitler's efforts.

Goebbels and Hitler had the same propaganda philosophy:

use every available means simultaneously and with full force. An intriguing part is that in those days, apart from radio, films and print media, there was hardly any other mass communication vehicle available, and yet the Nazi Party managed to influence most Germans and the world so effectively. Some of the techniques employed by them were as follows:

- **Speeches:** Goebbels knew that the spoken word or power of speech was more effective than written material. He, therefore, put together good speakers from the Nazi Party and managed them in a synchronized manner. The speakers were actually instructed on what to say! This brought consistency to the propaganda campaign.
- **Radio:** Radio was fully exploited by the propaganda machinery. Millions of government-subsidized radio sets were distributed to ensure that at least 70 per cent of the German population was accessible at any point of time. Moreover, these sets had a limited frequency range and could not receive foreign broadcasts. Therefore, Hitler was able to keep the Germans away from any counter-propaganda.
- **Posters:** The Germans created thousands of different posters during 1930–45, which had a great visual impact and were difficult to ignore. Each poster campaign was conceived with proper layouts, besides clear and specific messages. Even in the pre-war period, Hitler used election posters that portrayed him as the saviour of Germany. Using symbolic imagery effectively, posters depicting German might were pasted across the country. These posters made Jews a punching bag for the Soviets, the Americans and the British.

- **Sports:** Hitler also took serious note of how Americans promoted their sports and adapted it cleverly to his own propaganda techniques. He learnt about this from Ernst 'Putzi' Hanfstängl, an American expatriate who told him how Americans created a great atmosphere at football games and whipped up frenzy through blaring music, group cheering and chants against the opponent. German political rhetoric was generally dry and intellectual. A quick learner, Hitler transformed the great Nuremberg Rallies into glorified, football half-time shows. Appeals of blood and soil, or honour and pride of the fatherland, found more favour with people than pure ideology. He also borrowed the idea of using images or pictures that attracted people. Hitler's regime accordingly built huge arenas that could hold as many as 4,00,000 people. Hundreds of strong searchlights were installed around them, which, when lit up vertically into the dark night sky, could be seen from as far as 100 kilometres away. Sir Neville Henderson, a noted British political figure, called one such event the 'Cathedral of Light'. When Hitler spoke at rallies (which were more like military parades), loudspeakers were installed throughout the city so that no one missed what he said. Huge swastika-bearing flags were plastered behind the stage to create an electrifying effect. People actually participated psychologically in those moments of solidarity as if already catapulted into victory.
- **Films:** All Nazi propaganda films were produced with care. Leni Riefenstahl's 1935 film *Triumph of the Will* was a powerful documentation of the Nuremberg Rally. Its cast included Hitler, Goebbels, military leader Hermann Göring and a member of the Nazi Party, Heinrich Himmler. The

period of 1933–45 was when a large number of propaganda films were made by brilliant German directors, all set to numb the minds of Germans through the make-believe fantasy of Germany's might. These movies also portrayed that a huge wrong was done to them by neighbouring countries.

- **Books:** Books can be as powerful a source as films or radio for spreading an ideology. Besides having a long shelf life, they help in reinforcing the ideology since readers can share or refer to them repeatedly. If written well, a book can have a telling effect on the audience, so much so that it can make faithful disciples of a philosophy or the philosopher. *Mein Kampf* is a classic case in point, which sold over 5 million copies within a short period of its release and continues to sell all over the world even today! Books aligned to the Nazi ideology highlighted the geopolitical angle through atlases and demonstrated how, encircled by other nations, Germany could be overrun any time. They elaborated disadvantages of being a land-locked country with no access to the sea, hence proposing the expansion of Germany to reach territories with coastal access. Such thoughts and theories were even planted in most textbooks, across all age groups. Textbooks published during Hitler's regime also laid strong emphasis on the importance of studying physics, chemistry, technology and research for military use. They would carry stories of the greatness of the German people, besides showering open praise for the Nazi philosophy. English translations of such books would also be made available in occupied territories, to influence maximum people.

- **Magazines:** All magazines were given clear guidelines on what to publish, what to avoid and what would attract severe Nazi crackdown. The ideology that the Germans were pure and the Jews were a race of defectives was expected to appear in the maximum number of articles or features. Throughout the Second World War, German magazines would have articles that even urged German women to produce more children, ostensibly to further the race!
- **Music:** Germany produced some of the very best music composers of the world. Ludwig Van Beethoven was a music composer, pianist and a legend and so was Johann Sebastian Bach. The Nazi party utilized the services of the best available music composers to create propaganda music.
- **Symbols:** Hitler and Goebbels taught the world the meaning and impact of symbolism, and used a modified form of the swastika as their symbol. The swastika originated in ancient Indian and means an 'auspicious object'. Even today, followers of Hinduism use it as a traditional religious symbol. A modified form of the swastika was used as Nazi symbolism in almost every visual propaganda tool like armbands, badges and flags. In *Mein Kampf*, Hitler defines his own interpretation of the swastika flag—it was designed to give the Nazis a distinctive and recognizable logo. The Nazi flag was designed using the colours red, white and black of the German Empire. The red represented the social idea of the Nazi movement, the white disc represented the national idea, and the black swastika emblem represented the mission of the struggle for the victory of the 'Aryan race'. Hitler particularly admired the visual effect of the red flag used by Marxists (Communists) and therefore was keen to have the entire background as red for the Nazi flag.

The colour contrast of red, white and black was used with spectacular effect. When used with lighting, it created a lot of visual appeal and excitement in the audience. During grand stage events, huge swastika symbols were used as backdrops. At times, three or more flags were hung from top to bottom, with the swastika in the middle, to create an effect of grandeur. The Nazis used another symbol, the Garuda, prominently. It is a large eagle-like bird that features in ancient Hindu scriptures like the Ramayana. While the military wore this eagle spreading its wings on a swastika as a cap badge, Schutzstaffel or SS officers—a handpicked lot of men faithful only to Hitler and feared by all—also wore a skull badge to symbolize fear and death. People who wore the latter felt a sense of tremendous power. However, the people who had to confront such men were scared to death, since the SS was trained to be completely ruthless.

Hitler, thus, prepared Germany for war through his perfectly managed propaganda. He justified the invasion of Poland with his first big lie, generating a national and international propaganda campaign accusing and blaming the Polish government of tolerating and even organizing the ethnic cleansing of Germans living in Poland by the use of force and violence. On 22 August 1939, Hitler told his generals, 'I will provide a propagandistic "Casus Beth" (justification for act of war). Its credibility does not matter. The victor will not be asked whether he told the truth.' On 1 September, Germany invaded Poland and started the Second World War.

During the war, Hitler's propaganda strategy changed a number of times. It was timed, planned and executed as

Germany made or broke alliances with other countries. As they say, in politics, there are no permanent friends or enemies. Until the conclusion of the Battle of Stalingrad in February 1943, the thrust of the German propaganda was that German soldiers were humane, whereas the British and Americans were barbaric. After the battle, which saw the defeat of Nazi forces at the hands of the Soviets, it was time to change the propaganda strategy and hit out at them.

By 1940, Germany had almost won the war and therefore, felt no urgency for using new weapons. Although German scientists had researched pilotless planes and robot bombs since the 30s, Germany never really felt their need until 1942, when it started losing ground on all major fronts. Hence, during 1942–43, the V1 rockets (or rocket bombs) were developed and manufactured rather hastily, primarily targeted for use against the British. Time now was ripe to unveil this new ammunition to the German people in order to raise their sagging morale, besides trying to scare the British and Americans, who, by then, had started tasting a few victories. The V1, and subsequently developed V2 rockets, had deadly payloads of 2,000 pounds of explosives. Known as the weapons of vengeance in the propaganda parlance, the Germans were ready to fire the V2 rockets that reached the target in 4 seconds and at a speed of 3,500 mph! Despite firing almost 1,000 rockets targeted at London, Germany achieved only 50 per cent success, but this still had a positive impact on the German morale and did scare the Allies.

By the middle of 1944, Germany started facing frequent defeats. Therefore, when it started losing out on almost every front, Hitler's propaganda machinery began to focus on the hardship aspect of war and held that victory was not an easy goal.

There is a popular military phrase: 'Bullshit Baffles Brains'. Hitler and his Nazi party certainly managed to create enough bullshit to sway an arguably intelligent German race, which not only voted them to power but also followed them right through the long and dark years of the bloodiest war in human history. Shock and awe can paralyse the willpower of an adversary. Unfortunately, Hitler applied the technique on his own people. Goebbels was also instrumental in bringing Hitler to power by using mob frenzy and by manipulating the feelings of the German people. He used all available means to instil the concept of *one leader* in Germans, installing Hitler as a veritable god and a messiah of the Germans meant to rule the world. He placed his undeniable intelligence and understanding of mass psychology at the service of Hitler and the Nazi party.

Germany was eventually defeated and destroyed, but one cannot deny that Hitler and his comrades created one of the most formidable propaganda machines ever devised.

British Propaganda

During and before the Second World War, German propaganda under Hitler and the Nazi Party was directed at creating a warlike environment in the minds of Germans and build a revenge-seeking mindset in every German living in Germany as well as abroad. In a way, Hitler built his war on this proactive propaganda.

The British, on the other hand, appealed to their people to fight a just war and presented it as a struggle based on the issue of good vs. evil. The basic theme was to resist the German invasion and liberate the occupied countries from the clutches of Hitler's regime. They created the Ministry of

Information to coordinate the propaganda effort during the entire war and relied on their sound worldwide news network to reach out to create a sympathy wave and pull more allies into the war.

They also employed traditional media like newspapers, magazines and films to motivate their people and influence them towards supporting the war effort. The British also used the radio extensively to reach out to their audience as they wanted to keep the morale of their people high and wanted public participation in the war effort. Propaganda was used to motivate people to participate in a range of activities such as growing their own vegetables in the backyard to donating scrap metal in the form of old pots and pans, which could be used for making weapons.

American Propaganda

Patriotism and fighting for a just cause was also the central theme of American propaganda throughout the period of their involvement in the Second World War. Propaganda was used to muster American public opinion and garner participation with a commitment to the Allies' victory. Campaigns were engineered and conducted to sell war bonds, which urged Americans to save more so that funds could be mobilized for war effort. In the beginning, the American government was not in favour of propaganda, which they opined was a tool for dictators and fascist regimes. But gradually, the American media persuaded the government to adopt it, because without this, it would be impossible to garner public support for a war being fought in Europe. Once the Americans were onto it, they went all guns blazing to exploit every available medium to the hilt. The major thrust was industrial production for the war effort, military recruitment and conservation of resources. The propaganda also focused on duty, honour and patriotism in order to keep the Americans engaged in the war effort.

American propaganda became very aggressive as well as effective after the Pearl Harbour attack by the Japanese. It relied heavily on the atrocities committed by the Japanese on American soldiers. 'Remember Pearl Harbour' became a popular slogan to remind people of that unforgiveable act on the part of the Axis powers, especially the Japanese. Americans probably used more posters than any other country involved in the war. More than 2,00,000 differently designed posters were used during the period from 1941 to 1945. They also used films to motivate their people. *Why We Fight* is a series of seven documentary films created by Frank Capra, which depicted the perils of Hitler's victory and urged people to put all their might behind the struggle against German invasion. President Roosevelt released these for the consumption of the public and at the request of Winston Churchill, they were screened for the public in England too.

Animation got a shot in the arm during the Second World War, especially after the Pearl Harbour attack. Earlier seen as childlike stuff for mere entertainment, the American army used this as a tool to train their recruits and motivate the ordinary American citizen. Walt Disney Studios was a major player making such films. Movies were a satire on the Japanese and Germans, especially Hitler, who was shown in poor light and as good as doomed.

Radio was extensively used for war propaganda in America. Some of the popular series were broadcast throughout the world. Roosevelt frequently addressed Americans through a popular programme called *Fireside Chats*. As a result of all this, the American advertising industry matured in its approach and intent and found a respectable place in the hearts and minds of the American people.

The Allies won the Second World War and the world order quickly changed to a bipolar power equation, where the US and the USSR found themselves directly pitted against each other, though together, they had both fiercely fought a hot war against Germany and its allies for several years and come out as winners.

The Cold War Propaganda

The American and Soviet war machinery had matured and evolved during 1939–45. During this period, the world got its new weapon of mass destruction—the A-bomb. Though they couldn't engage in a direct confrontation with each other, they fought what was subsequently known as the Cold War.

Both the Americans and the Soviets had strong ideologies that were literally poles apart. There was no way to reconcile or find any room to agree to disagree. By 1950, both were nuclear powers and resorted to propaganda to promote their ideologies at home as well as abroad. Americans went all out to project the capitalistic-democratic way of governance as the best way forward, and probably the only way forward. It was done with little subtlety and Americans went ahead to propagate their capitalistic society and lifestyle through films, music, literature and television. Americans and the world were told that there was no better place to be than America. The film and creative fraternity played ball and the government thereafter produced less of propaganda content themselves and let the private industry do the rest by incorporating the American capitalistic way of life in their creations. American policymakers were quick to criticize communism as a way of living and as an ideology. Propaganda was the most dependable tool to keep communism at bay from the rest of the world and stop its aggression in Eastern Europe. Lyndon B. Johnson, then vice president of the US, said in 1961, 'A nation that knows how to popularize cornflakes and luxury automobiles ought to be able to tell the world the simple truth about what it is doing and why it is doing it.'

The Soviets, on the other hand, depended on an 'iron curtain', which allowed them to hide from the world their methods to deal with their people at home, most of which were coercive to bring their subjects in line. Marxist-Leninist ideology was promoted throughout the USSR and the Communist Party heavily depended on propaganda using all available means and channels. They ensured that propaganda and censorship went hand in hand and their methods were omnipresent. The ideological spin of 'equality' and 'comradeship' was visible in every publication and every institution that mattered, right from the schools to workplaces. It promoted collective living and rejected the idea of parents bringing up their children as they wanted to inculcate nationalism in the youth. The KGB was omnipresent and those not toeing the official line were severely punished.

Soviet propaganda was implemented with an iron hand, and failed to win the hearts of the Soviets. Propaganda means to touch and win the hearts of people through emotional and motivational methods and not to push dictum down their throats. While American propaganda reached hearts, the Soviets could only drum it into the heads of their people. The Americans not only successfully won over their own people but were also able to reach out to the Soviet diaspora behind the iron curtain, using subtle yet convincing ways.

The novel *Doctor Zhivago* makes an interesting case. When the USSR denied permission to Boris Pasternak, a well-respected Russian author, to publish his book *Doctor Zhivago*, Americans were quick to capitalize on this opportunity. Though the book was published in Italian by Giangiacomo Feltrinelli, an Italian publisher, Americans got it published in Russian and sneaked it into the hands of the Soviet masses, making them wonder why such a great novel written by one of their countrymen was available only abroad. This was a subtle way to show communism in poor light in front of the Soviet citizens. The novel got huge publicity because of this and later Pasternak won the Nobel Prize for his contribution to literature.

Marketing and Politics: The Subtler, the Better

Propaganda in totalitarian regimes like China and Russia is implemented inefficiently and most of the times, is ineffective in garnering favourable public opinion. It is too blatant to be taken as true by the public and as soon as you read the first line in a magazine or newspaper, you realize that it is state-sponsored. People quickly get disinterested with lousy state-sponsored speeches that talk ill of other countries' ideologies. Nobody believes the state, but no one wants to cross paths with the state police or communist authority either. Though it remains in their heads, it never reaches their hearts. Americans did it the smart way.

The Second World War was like a shot in the arm for the American advertising industry. After the war, Americans wanted a respite and probably a better way of life. American advertising and marketing relied heavily on sexuality, a sense of pride in owning quality products and the fear of being left behind. Advertising gurus therefore created demand among American men through advertisements that showed men in demand. Women were wooed by clever advertisement campaigns capitalizing on theirs fears of inadequacy and failure. Advertisements were created around basic emotions like lust, fear, greed and envy, as no one buys morality and ethics. It is here that the communist propaganda failed—they talked of collectivism and equality, which no one was prepared to buy. Each one is for himself as people don't want to remain equal; that's the basis of competition and aspiration.

After the war, the American government borrowed ideas from private advertising companies to influence Americans and the rest of the world, basing their propaganda strategy entirely on emotional appeal, and cutting out the dry logic and rationale.

Lobbying, Branding and Advertising

In the last two decades, marketing and advertising have taken centre stage in every business proposition. Earlier, this substantial sum was hardly ever spent on marketing and branding.

Large corporations to the smallest of startups invest time and money to strategize how to position and make their product visible in the marketplace through advertisements. A decade ago, cinema was promoted through hoardings and banners alone. Today, every movie is being promoted through TV and on social media platforms. Actors spend substantial time to promote their films by travelling to different towns and conducting live shows. Great films and good products can fail if they are not marketed properly with enough finance to back the marketing and advertising effort.

Companies attract talent by branding themselves as 'the best place to work'. Every airline, hotel, restaurant, school, college, luxury or non-luxury product is trying to make a place in the customer's mind. Social media has become a new game changer and has created social media marketing, a new business avenue. There are a large number of media options available and one has to choose a 'media mix' wisely, according to the audience, budget and product.

The tools may have changed, but the basic principles of marketing and advertising remain the same—a derivative of old-school propaganda techniques.

Mood and Times

While strategizing propaganda, the mood of the nation and the current times need to be considered. The age-old maxim, 'Which way does the wind blow?' says it all. After the First World War, the Treaty of Versailles was a sore point for every German and was fresh in their minds. There was a mood to take revenge. Revenge and hatred are very strong emotions, which Hitler was quick to encash upon. Instead of boring political speeches, he based his propaganda on rhetoric and imagery. In the hearts of Germans, he created a fear of the Allies and played on the huge war reparation costs that were slapped on Germany. His propaganda disapproved the seemingly unfair treaty that was carved out by the rest of the world against German people. As for pride, he gave them the hope of being the best race in the world.

American politicians learnt pretty early that elections can be won by swaying public opinion in their favour. And the way forward was to cleverly weave emotional appeal into their presidential campaigns. A lot went into crafting and drafting presidential speeches and one-liners that went well with the mood of the nation. These one-liners were often reasonably achievable, and so hazy that no one would bother to dissect them. 'Yes, we can!' got America to vote for Obama—just three pretty words! President Roosevelt also played on the feeling of fear and promoted a concept of social security, which no one could oppose. Every advertisement suggested and adequately demonstrated that if you didn't get social security, you would live your old age in a miserable condition. Therefore, America rallied behind him. Propaganda is about creating so much noise that a person who reasons otherwise is made to look stupid. When the attack on Pearl Harbour happened, America was wooed into the war by the government. The handful of people who opposed were snubbed and labeled as isolationists.

People have been bombarded with certain buzzwords by management gurus who have been able to numb even the mightiest of intellectual minds. Paradigm shift, synergy, stakeholders, transformation, new world order and transparency are some of the most commonly used ones. Often someone with whom the public can relate vis-à-vis a product is hired to sell that product. That is why celebrities, who are often fit, endorse health foods. Who is going to buy a health drink if the MD of that company comes on a TV show to endorse it? Likewise, a lesser-known actor pretending to be a middle-class person can endorse products like washing powder more effectively than a film star, as the public knows that the latter doesn't do such chores on a regular basis.

Propaganda Today: Terrorism and War

Several times in the history of warfare, politicians have taken their countries to war by projecting a false threat through the use of propaganda. The Iraq War is a case in point. George Bush made Americans believe that Saddam Hussein had close ties with the Al-Qaeda and was in possession of weapons of mass destruction including chemical and biological ones. It was also proclaimed that he intended to use these weapons against America and its allies. The American government simultaneously manipulated evidence and created an unopposable argument through well-orchestrated rhetoric. It was more likely a revenge for the 9/11 attack. 'Al-Qaeda' and 'Iraq' were the key expressions used effectively throughout the campaign. The chorus was so strong that during the middle of the Iraq invasion, many Americans started believing that Saddam Hussein was actually responsible for the 9/11 attack.

For a propaganda campaign to be successful, the 'threat' also needs to be endorsed by other people in authority. President Bush was not the only one who claimed that Iraq possessed such weapons, his entire top brass batted for him, including Vice President Richard Cheney, Secretary of State Collin Powell, National Security Adviser Condoleezza Rice and Defense Secretary Donald Rumsfeld. The media played ball and Bush was able to rope in the UK, Australia and Poland into this conflict where many lost their lives.

The methods of influencing people have remained the same over the last 100 years. Today, the media is omnipresent and all-accessible. Rationality says that the common man cannot be duped by propaganda, but we must realize that even if we are alert and stay connected, we are fed an overload of information on a daily basis through multiple channels of communications, and it often becomes difficult to separate the wheat from the chaff.

7

Surprise and Deception: Hit When He Least Expects It

> *'Let your plans be dark and impenetrable as night, and when you move, fall like a thunderbolt.'*
> —Sun Tzu

The Importance of the Element of Surprise in Warfare

Surprise and deception are as old as war itself and are not only crucial but enduring elements of diplomacy and warfare. They are primarily psychological phenomena, rooted in human nature and, therefore, inherent in the very character of force and diplomacy. Surprise plays an integral role in a battle or military operation conducted over a large theatre of war and is often seen as an 'operational game changer.' It provides an overwhelming advantage at the tactical, strategic and even political levels.

A stratagem or plan lies at the foundation of every attempt to surprise. It implies a concealed objective, one that makes the person being deceived draw erroneous results from the actions of the deceiver. At the tactical level, a commander can hit the enemy where he least expects. It is like a clever boxer who uses a punch when the opponent probably expects a jab. When applied at the right place and at the right time, surprise rattles the adversary because it gives him very little reaction time—and that is the most important outcome of springing a surprise.

Military commanders carry out a recce of the situation, the enemy's preparedness and the possible reactions the adversary commander could take in response to their action.

This way they condition their minds and expect the enemy to behave according to their own calculations within their own framework. If the enemy is able to do something different from this assumption (he is able to spring a surprise by this unexpected reaction), it causes panic and the inability to react on time appropriately. Surprise and deception, therefore, work in the minds of the enemy commanders.

If you can choose a time and place according to your terms, then you can fight the battle on your terms. It can be achieved by use of a feint. Here you make the enemy believe that you are attacking at one particular location, which makes him focus on that location, while you actually attack in a different location, which obviously would be weakly defended. You know where and when the battle will take place, whereas the enemy is unaware. Surprise can be achieved at the operational, strategic as well at technological levels.

Changing Scenarios: Different Shades, Different Times

Surprise attacks and guiles were practised even by biblical-era warriors and kings. From ancient Persia, Greece and Rome, through the double world wars and the first decades of the 21st century, nations and non-state actors have both used surprise and deception and fallen victim to them.

Before the 20th century, soldiers fought battles mostly on foot or on horseback. The ability to manoeuvre was limited by the speed of the marching infantry and horses determined the highest attainable speed in a battle. In such battlefields, the element of surprise was an important winning parameter. Commanders at all levels tried to outwit their adversaries during all the major wars of the 19th century. Deceit, deception and surprise were therefore used in all major military campaigns during the Napoleonic Wars (1803-1815), the American Civil War (1861-1865) and the Franco-Prussian War (1870-1871).

Speed and lethality took a quantum leap during the two world wars, primarily because of mechanical transport, tanks, aircraft, ships and the tremendous firepower of guns and small arms. In such a scenario, surprise and deception had a bigger impact on tactics and strategy as the new generation of weaponry compressed reaction time for belligerent commanders.

The Cold War started between the Soviets and the Americans immediately after the Second World War. Nuclear weapons and space-based ballistic missiles brought about a marked change in weapon systems. The lethality and destructive power of nuclear weapons was unimaginable, and this brought a paradigm shift in strategic thinking. Space-based missile systems also had an intercontinental range and the time of flights was measured in minutes. Space-based monitoring systems and sensors could track an enemy missile attack in seconds. This compressed the reaction time tremendously. Integrating all these together created a formidable system that made the operational scenario very complex. In such a scenario, space-based sensor systems became essential to prevent a strategic surprise. Both adversaries need to have such systems in place. The Cold War was literally a cat-and-mouse chase, where both opponents were trying to not get surprised by the other all the time.

Today, each nation state needs to maintain 'technological parity' in order to remain at par with others. Strategic advantage can be gained by developing and acquiring a new family of weapon systems without the adversary knowing about it. This, in effect, is a technological surprise. Such revolutionary or breakthrough systems are not easy to come by and extremely difficult to hide from the enemy. In the past, radios, radars, rockets, space-based missiles and atom bombs were the game changers. Now, any weapon system that can escape scrutiny from space will be the ultimate winner. It is, in a way, a 'technology race'. In practice, however, it is harder to spring a technological surprise than an operational surprise, due to the long turnaround time required for R&D for an operationally viable military system.

Deception: A Key Principle

Most military operations employ different means to achieve surprise. One of the key means is deception. Sun Tzu wrote around 500 BCE, 'All warfare is based on deception!' He was one of the first to envision it as a principle of war. This was accepted as a major means to achieve results with much lesser force throughout the history of warfare.

The sole purpose of deception is to mislead, misguide and outwit the enemy, by making him believe what you want him to believe. Dr Michael Handel has given one of the clearest definitions of deception: 'A purposeful attempt by the deceiver to manipulate the perceptions of the target's decision-maker in order to gain competitive advantage.'[11]

---

[11]Merritt, R.C. (1994). *Surprise and Deception in Joint Warfare*. Naval War College, Newport, R.I., Department Of Operations.

Today, deception is considered a force multiplier at the tactical as well as strategic level. It can rapidly yield decisive results with minimal casualties. Some of the axioms for planning and executing deception target the mind of the decision-maker by reinforcing his beliefs. The deceptors use multiple sources to authenticate facts, monitor the effect of their actions on the enemy's mind and do it over a sustained period, thereby ensuring effective deception.

There are several ways, techniques and methods to deceive the enemy. Broadly, the major ones are physical, diplomatic, technical and electronic. Physical methods include movement of critical weapon systems, large movement of troops and displaying training activities like war games, to give an impression that something is brewing and some action is imminent.

Diplomatic efforts for deception are in terms of making favourable pacts, treaties and maintaining dialogue with the enemy to conceal your actual intent. Spies and moles play an important part in planting information in the minds of decision-makers to make them think the way you want them to. They also try to extract the enemy's intent.

Today, technology and electronics play a very important role in deception, and electronic warfare is a major means of deceiving the enemy. Modern weapons as well as command and control systems become more and more dependent on electronic communication, thus becoming more susceptible to enemy highjack. Spurious radiations, deceptive data flow and deliberate leakage of false information to the enemy can be a very cost-effective means of achieving surprise and winning a war.

Military Campaigns Before the Two World Wars Where Surprise Was Used to Win

The Trojan War (1260–1180 BCE)

This is one of the most popular and perhaps the oldest example of the element of surprise. The Greeks and the Trojans were engaged in a long-drawn-out conflict, and the former managed to devise a cunning trick to mount a surprise attack on the Trojans, by way of a simple plan.

The Greeks built a huge hollow wooden horse that could hide a number of their soldiers. They left the horse outside the city gates of Troy and pretended to desert the war. They even left a Greek called Sinon behind to convince the Trojans that this was a gift from the Greeks and would bring them good luck if they moved it into the city of Troy. Some Trojans were not convinced, but somehow Sinon convinced the decision-makers to take the wooden horse inside the city. The warriors who were hiding inside the horse came out at night and opened the gates of the city, allowing the Greek army an easy entry into Troy and eventually defeating the Trojans who were taken completely by surprise.

The Battle of Trenton (1776)

During the American Revolution, the Battle of Trenton was a small but important battle, which turned the tide in favour of the American forces. It was fought between the American Continental Army led by George Washington and the British forces along with their Hessian soldiers. At that point, the American forces were facing problems of low morale, lack of military hardware and severe shortage of soldiers.

General Washington made all his moves in such a way that he could take the enemy by surprise. He planted a spy in the enemy camp to spread a rumour that the American forces were in total disarray and would never attempt to attack. Therefore, the British felt safe and never positioned their long-distance outposts or patrolling to monitor any incoming attack. A three-pronged attack was then planned and Washington lead 2,400 men across an icy river in the middle of snow and rain on Christmas day. They attacked the city of Trenton around 8 a.m. the next day and caught the British unaware. They thus captured a large number of enemy soldiers as well as arms and ammunition.

Operation Barbarossa (22 June–5 December 1941)

Operation Barbarossa, the German invasion of the Soviet Union, began the largest and most costly campaign in military history. It was planned as a blitzkrieg to win Germany its Lebensraum (living space). Three main factors contributed to Hitler's resolution of attacking the USSR. First, one of the biggest concerns was that Britain might close ranks with the USSR, entice the US into the war and thus attack Germany on two fronts. By defeating the Soviets, Hitler could eliminate the British threat. Second, Hitler contended that national socialism was incompatible with 'an Eastern Europe filled with Jews.' He opined that the Soviets were the most inferior race of slaves. And third, the Germans always felt that they had insufficient land and their policy of Lebensraum was therefore well enshrined in the political philosophy of the Nazi Party. Hitler viewed the USSR as a 'breadbasket,' a huge landmass that could give Germany the required space. The purges and mass executions of Soviet military leaders and the widespread dissatisfaction with the repressive Stalinist regime made this area ripe for taking. Though Hitler had his expansionist plans well laid out in front of the Germans and the rest of the world, he cleverly managed to keep his intentions of waging a war against Russia a closely guarded secret. He wanted to first handle the rest of Europe before taking on the Soviets, and wanted to secure the confidence of the Soviet political leadership by signing a treaty. In August 1939, Germany and the USSR signed a non-aggression pact, which assured Joseph Stalin that Germany would not attack them.

It was sometime in the middle of 1941 that Hitler wanted to attack the USSR, and mobilization of German forces for this large-scale operation had begun much in advance. Stalin, who had been informed about the impending invasion by his intelligence network, refused to believe them. He blindly trusted Hitler. He was also prepared to accept Hitler's explanation about the presence of a large number of German troops near the Soviet border as 'a move to keep German troops out of the range of British air strikes'. Stalin was so convinced about Hitler's good intentions that he ordered not to fire on any German planes that entered the Soviet air space, which he took as accidental cases of violation. The Soviets were completely unprepared for the attack due to Stalin's obstinacy.

On 22 June 1941, the German forces launched a surprise attack with more than 3 million troops across 2,900 km, from German-controlled Romania, Poland and Finland. It was the largest surprise attack in the history of warfare, which involved 3.8 million German frontline soldiers, 7,200 pieces of artillery and guns, more than 3,000 tanks and close to 3,000 German aircraft. The surprise was successful as the Soviets had been caught unprepared and the German army advanced more than 200 miles inside their territory within a week. Operation Barbarossa was a spectacular example of lightning warfare.

Though the Germans initially had an upper hand, due to the severe climatic conditions of the Russian winter, the rest of the German campaign took a major beating. Germany lost 900,000 men while the Soviets suffered 40,00,000 casualties. On 5 December 1941, after five months of fierce fighting, Germany lost the war on the Eastern front.

The Pearl Harbour Attack (7 December 1941)

> *'Yesterday, Dec. 7, 1941, a date which will live in infamy, the United States of America was suddenly and deliberately attacked by naval and air forces of the Empire of Japan.'*
> —Franklin D. Roosevelt

The Pearl Harbour attack is another surgically well-conducted surprise attack in the history of warfare, and has been characterized as a 'catastrophe' and 'the worst military disaster in American history'. It was a preplanned attack by the Imperial Japanese Navy on the American Naval Base at Pearl Harbour, on the island of Oahu in Hawaii. This operation was undertaken by Japan to prevent the US pacific fleet from interfering with Japanese expansionist plans to attack the Southeast Asian countries of Malaya, the Philippines, Hong Kong and Singapore. This blow brought the US into the war, which then exploded worldwide, with fronts not only in Europe and the Atlantic but also in Asia and the Pacific.

The attack had taken Americans by total surprise, as they had no inkling about such a military strike, which occurred on a Sunday morning. The Japanese used a naval force comprising six aircraft carriers, two main battleships and several destroyers and cruisers to launch 414 fighters and bomber aircraft on the American ships, aircraft and military hardware harboured in the naval base. They reached within 200 miles of Oahu at the dawn of 7 December and the first wave of aircraft comprising bombers, fighters and torpedo bombers took off at 6 a.m. to reach their target by 7.55 a.m. The raid commenced around 8 a.m. and was carried out in two waves, causing huge losses to the American fleet, which was like a sitting duck for the Japanese aircraft.

The Americans lost six battleships with more than a dozen ships damaged. As luck would have it, the three American aircraft carriers that were to be the primary target of the Japanese raid were not in the harbour. However, most of the other American aircraft had been parked on the airfield and the naval base lost 188 aircraft with an almost equal number badly damaged. America also lost more than 2,400 men in this swiftly conducted operation, which lasted just two hours. The Japanese losses, on the other hand, were minimal—less than 30 aircraft, five submarines and 70 casualties.

The attack was so well planned and executed that the Japanese naval task force headed back for Japan by 1 p.m. They had rehearsed this raid for a year on a mock-up model and had achieved an efficiency of 80 per cent before attempting the actual strike on ground. Surprise could be attributed to the American intelligence failure as well, which could not interpret the data available to them through radio intercepts months before.

This pussyfoot attack caused Americans great embarrassment. The humiliation was more than the loss of men and material. This one operation changed the course of the war as America entered it, declaring their first strike on

Japan. A sleeping giant had been awoken, and the losses at Pearl Harbour had been more than made good, with not just Japan but also Germany and its allies paying a heavy price.

American economist Murray N. Rothbard said, 'A detailed analysis of the Pearl Harbour attack brings about inevitable lessons as to the uncertainties of human judgement and the eccentricities in personal conduct that control the outbreak of wars. Not only that, they design the destinies of human civilization at the wake of the Nuclear Era. The personal and political ambitions, professional stereotypes, public deceit and the credibility gap, and ruts and grooves of thinking and action, if repeated, would destroy the human civilization.'

The Six-Day War (5-10 June 1967)

The June 1967 war between Arab and Israel was a milepost moment in the history of the modern Middle East. In six quick days, the Israelis defeated the Arabs and seized giant portions of territory including the West Bank, East Jerusalem, the Gaza Strip, the Sinai Peninsula and the Golan Heights.

Since the 1948 Arab-Israel War, Israel and its Arab neighbours had been involved in a long-standing dispute that heightened to dangerous levels by mid-1967. Under the leadership of their president, Gamal Abdel Nasser, Egypt mobilized its forces in the Sinai Peninsula along Israel's border. On 30 May, Jordan and Egypt signed a defense pact and roped in Iraq to deploy troops in Jordan. Anticipating a major conflict, Israel widened its cabinet by constituting a national unity government on 1 June and decided to go to war against the Arabs.

Though highly outnumbered, Israel decided to use speed, stealth, secrecy and surprise to defeat the four nations that had ganged up against it. At the time of going to war, the

Israeli armed forces had 264,000 combatants and less than 300 aircraft, as compared to the 547,000 combatants and 975 aircraft of their adversaries.

On 5 June 1967, Israel launched a surprise attack on Egypt's air force, destroying most of it. Operation Focus, as it was known, began at 7.45 a.m., using all of Israel's 200 combat aircraft and leaving only 12 behind for local air defense. Israeli aircraft flew over the Mediterranean Sea and some took the route over the Red Sea and flew below Egyptian radar cover at a very low altitude to avoid detection. The surprise was total and the speed unimaginable. To incapacitate the enemy air power, the Israeli air force used rocket-assisted warheads known as 'the Durandal anti-runway warhead', a penetration bomb that was made under a French-Israel weapon programme. Dropped from parachutes, the rockets would drive the warheads into the pavement of the airstrip, creating massive sinkholes and craters that could not be repaired easily. Hence, the runways were disabled and virtually no Egyptian aircraft could take off. All 500 aircraft were then blown up by the next wave of Israeli aircraft within the first three hours, such that 18 Egyptian airfields were crippled for the rest of the war. By noon, the Syrian and Jordanian air force had also been destroyed.

The Israeli air force not only used the element of surprise, but also rehearsed and prepared the pilots and the ground crew to become considerably more efficient and effective than their enemy, thus combining surprise with speed. They practised rapid refuelling, rearming and refitting of aircraft returning from a sortie to take off again in just 7 minutes and 30 seconds to hit at the enemy targets. Each pilot was doing four sorties a day as compared to the capability of one or two in a day by the Arabs.

Operation Entebbe (1976)

Operation Entebbe was probably the fastest clandestine military operation in the history of warfare. On 4 July 1976, a team of 100 Israeli commandos managed to rescue more than 100 hostages from the clutches of terrorists across a distance of 4,000 km. Political will, detailed planning, secrecy and bold action culminated into a military operation that surprised not only the terrorists and their supporters but also the whole world. The raid is remembered today as one of Israel's finest and the reason the then unknown Bibi Netanyahu was hailed a national hero.

On 27 June 1976, an Air France plane with 248 passengers and 12 crew members took off from Tel Aviv airport for Paris. Unfortunately, the plane had been highjacked and rerouted to Entebbe in Uganda by four terrorists belonging to the Popular Front for the Liberation of Palestine. The highjackers wanted 53 pro-Palestinian militants held in Israeli prisons to be freed in exchange of the hostages. All the hostages were moved into the airport building and within a day, the non-Israeli hostages were released and sent to Paris, leaving behind 102 Israelis in captivity. Moreover, the Ugandan government headed by the dictator, Idi Amin, supported the Palestinian highjackers.

The Israeli government tried all diplomatic channels to negotiate the release of hostages, but nothing seemed to work in that situation. They even tried to persuade the Ugandan president and approached him through an old acquaintance of his, a retired army officer called Colonel Baruch Bar-Lev, who had known Amin for many years. Once this effort also failed, the Israeli cabinet, on the evening of 3 July, took the decision to go for military action.

The task force had to be transported by air to a distance of 4,000 km with a plan to neutralize the terrorists and rescue the hostages in the shortest possible time. Four Lockheed C-130 Hercules aircraft along with two Boeings were required to conduct this operation. Israel did not have the capability of air fuelling these on the way and required a friendly African country en route, which would allow refuelling of these aircraft. They managed to persuade Kenya's President Jomo Kenyatta to help.

An accurate picture of the location of the hostages, the involvement of the Ugandan army and the number of terrorists was required to plan the operation. Mossad, the Israeli intelligence agency, gathered this information from the released hostages. To build a replica of the airport, they took the help of the Israeli company that had built it in 1960-70. All this was done with utmost secrecy and speed.

Lt Col. Yonatan Netanyahu led the main assault group of 29 commandos. There were three more groups for securing the airport and protecting their own aircraft while refuelling, for destroying the Ugandan aircraft parked at the airport and a reserve force that was also to be used to evacuate the hostages.

To deceive the Ugandan guards at the airport, the assault team used a black Mercedes and a Land Rover, which they had carried from Israel in the aircraft. These vehicles looked exactly like the ones used by their president Idi Amin while visiting the airport. The assault team entered the area where the hostages were lodged, announced on loudspeakers, 'Stay down, we are Israeli soldiers', and quickly eliminated all the terrorists. The hostages were whisked away to the standing rescue aircraft, which were ready to take off. Almost the entire fleet of Ugandan aircraft stationed at the airport was simultaneously destroyed to prevent them from pursuing.

The entire operation, from landing to takeoff, took 90 minutes, out of which the assault lasted for 30 minutes. Lt Col. Netanyahu was unfortunately fatally wounded. All highjackers and almost 45 Ugandan soldiers were killed. Three hostages were also killed and 10 had been wounded. All the aircraft returned back safely to Israel after a brief stopover at Nairobi, Kenya.

To quote British journalist Max Hastings, 'The day the hostages returned was the high-water mark of Israel's standing in the world. The success at Entebbe contributed to the exaltation of military capabilities and a downgrading of political compromise in Israel public life.'[12]

Operation Overlord (6 June 1944)

During the Second World War, the Battle of Normandy, which lasted from June to August 1944, resulted in the Allies' liberation of Western Europe from Nazi Germany's control. Codenamed 'Operation Overlord', it was the largest amphibious operation launched on 6 June 1944, where 160,000 Allied troops crossed the English Channel in one day. The assault was intended to first create a foothold on the French side of the English Channel, and then move on to recapture the rest of German-occupied Europe. Eventually, more than 3 million Allied troops entered France by the end of August and by the following spring, the Allies had defeated the Germans. This assault, also known as D-Day, required extensive planning. Prior to D-Day, the

---

[12]Shephard, B. (2015). 'Operation Thunderbolt: Flight 139 and the Raid on Entebbe review. Retrieved from https://www.theguardian.com/books/2015/jul/19/operation-thunderbolt-flight-139-raid-entebbe-review-saul-david

Allies conducted a large-scale deception campaign designed to mislead the Germans about the intended invasion target. The Normandy Landings have been called the beginning of the end of war in Europe.

The biggest challenge of this mammoth operation was to maintain secrecy. The element of surprise was the key to the success of an operation against an enemy who was well entrenched with fortified defenses across the French beaches. Since the war was in its fifth year, both sides were fully aware of each other's intentions. The Germans were expecting a major invasion across the channel, but were not sure about its location and timing. They were holding the entire coastline thinly, with a reserve mobile force to move and be deployed rapidly as and when the attack occurred. The Allied forces had to launch the attack from the English side of the channel and had limited options.

The Allies planned a detailed deception strategy that had been crafted well before the actual operation—Operation Bodyguard. Further, Operation Fortitude was the codename for the major part of Operation Bodyguard with the specific aim of deceiving the enemy regarding the date, time and location of the attack. This was further split into two components, which applied multiple methods to confuse the German high command until the day of the actual landings. Fortitude North was to make the Germans believe that the Allied invasion would attempt to take back German-occupied Norway. Simultaneously, Fortitude South used similar tactics to convince the enemy that the attack would come at Calais, hitting out at German-occupied France.

The actual attack at Normandy was to be undertaken by the 21st Army Group under General Montgomery. A fictitious force—the 1st US Army group under General George Patton—was created and positioned in Southeastern England to indicate the intention to attack Calais. Patton was a formidable general and therefore the Germans expected him to lead the 'main attack' at Calais, which was also the shortest stretch across the English Channel. To illustrate that the troop movement was indeed taking place within the fictitious army group, dummy tanks, trucks and landing craft were positioned near the coast. The reserve units were moved into the area to convince the Germans of a massive troop buildup. Fictitious radio traffic was passed between fictitious formations to portray intense activity that normally occurs before a massive invasion.

The Allies used German spies as double agents to pass wrong information to the German high command. Under Project Ultra, the Allies had, by then, been able to break German cipher codes and could decode most strategic German signal traffic. It was therefore easy for them to assess how successful their deception plan had been.

The deception plan for an operation of this magnitude was successful because of several reasons:

- A long-term detailed plan was in place much before the actual operation.
- The German spy network had been compromised and spies were extensively used by the Allies as double agents.
- The Allies were able to intercept, decode and decipher most of the communication between the German high command and the field commanders due to Project Ultra.
- Utmost secrecy was maintained at all levels to ensure that no information leaked out to the enemy.
- Even during the reconnaissance of the area, the Allied

aircraft did air photo reconnaissance of the entire coastline so that the Germans could not get to know the exact location of the invasion.
- Multiple methods had been used to confuse the enemy about the Allies' intentions.

The 9/11 Attack (2001)

On 11 September 2001, America woke up to witness one of the worst human tragedies when it was struck by a well-coordinated terrorist attack right in the heart of its homeland. Nineteen militants associated with the Islamic extremist group, Al-Qaeda, hijacked four airliners and conducted suicide attacks against targets in the US. Two of the planes were rammed into the towers of the World Trade Centre in New York City, a third hit the Pentagon right outside Washington D.C. and the fourth crashed in a field in Pennsylvania. Often referred to as 9/11, the attack resulted in massive death and destruction, killing around 3,000 people and causing an estimated loss of more than $10 billion to the infrastructure.

The plan was conceived in 1996 by Osama Bin Laden, leader of Al-Qaeda. They were acting in retaliation of America's support of Israel, its involvement in the Persian Gulf War and its military interference in the Middle East. In 1999, a group of four men from a sleeper group in Germany were selected by Bin Laden to go to America for this mission. Based out of Hamburg, the group started looking for a suitable flight school in the US to undergo flight training. They sent 50 to 60 emails to several schools to seek admission in March 2000.

Arriving in the month of May, they finally enrolled themselves at the Huffman Aviation School in Venice, Florida. No one suspected anything or could guess their intentions.

Secondary highjackers known as 'muscle highjackers' arrived in the spring of 2001. By July, they could coordinate the attack and also selected their targets. Four commercial airlines flying Boeings, en route California, were selected for this task because the planes were loaded with fuel for the long transcontinental journey. They were highjacked after takeoff early in the morning on 11 September.

A Boeing 767 was rammed into the North Tower of the World Trade Center at 8.46 a.m. in New York City. Exactly after 19 minutes, another rammed into the South Tower at 9.03 a.m. A Boeing 757 flew into the Pentagon at 9.37 a.m., roughly 34 minutes after the second hit. The fourth, a Boeing 755, crashed into a field in Shanksville, Pennsylvania, at 10.03 a.m. This was possibly heading for the White House but crashed on the way as the passengers resisted the terrorists onboard.

The surprise and shock were mammoth and everyone, including President George Bush, was baffled by this strike. No one had expected aircraft being used as missiles. What made them deadlier was that each carried more than 10,000 gallons of aviation fuel. When an aircraft flying at hundreds of miles per hour rams into a structure, it has a devastating effect, and both the towers collapsed within 90 minutes of the impact, crumbling like a pack of cards.

President George Bush later said, 'Terrorist attacks can shake the foundations of our biggest buildings, but they cannot touch the foundation of America. These acts shatter steel, but they cannot dent the steel of American resolve.' This attack triggered major US initiatives to combat terrorism worldwide.

Innovation Is an Essential Component of Surprise

For surprise to be effective, a plan has to be not only bold, but should also be different, new and unfamiliar for the enemy. It is, therefore, essential to be innovative while integrating the element of surprise in the overall operational plan. Deceit cannot be accomplished without creativity. For instance, the Trojan horse was a brilliant idea for hiding soldiers and positioning them within enemy territory. Similarly, the Durandal warhead was an innovative idea that nipped any possible counter-attacks in the bud. During the Entebbe raid, the masterstroke was the Israeli soldiers carrying a black Mercedes and a Land Rover that looked identical to the ones used by the Ugandan president. Hitler's 'non-aggression' treaty with the Soviets and feeding them conflicting inputs regarding troop movements near the Soviet border were innovative ways to keep the USSR at bay for as long as it was required. And finally, highjacking large fully loaded commercial aircraft of the enemy and ramming them into strategically important targets in their heartland was unimaginable. The terrorists also chose those buildings that were 'structurally suitable' for accruing maximum impact, collapsing under their own weight. Most importantly, all this gave them maximum bang—and without a buck!

Technological Surprise

In the matter of war, surprise is not only limited to operations and strategy, but manifests in the pursuit of new weapon systems and supporting technology. A plethora of new weapons and techniques in the hands of non-state actors threaten nations in fundamental ways, and they are always on the lookout for creating or upgrading weapons that are better than those possessed by the potential adversary. But it is not only important to have a better weapon than the enemy, but also to keep it under wraps, only to be used when the time is right.

The prerequisite of winning a war therefore lies in the ability to be able to spring a technological surprise on the enemy. Every new invention can become a game changer as soon as it is applied. One can take advantage of this surprise for as long as the enemy does not catch up and replicate or better it.

In the arms race, to retain military superiority, every country is looking for a killer app—one that can give a strategic edge over the adversary. A colossal amount is being constantly spent on the arms race by almost all those countries that wish to remain militarily relevant. Some projects that proved critical in creating new systems for warfare in recent times merit a look:

Project Manhattan

This was a massive project undertaken to produce the first atom bomb during the Second World War. It then cost the US $2 billion. Though the US was the only country with resources to develop the bomb, Germany and the USSR were close too. It was only after the Americans bombed Nagasaki and Hiroshima that the Soviets accelerated their nuclear programme, allocating large funds and employing many scientists. The first nuclear bomb was tested by them on 29 August 1949, making USSR the second nuclear power.

Project Manhattan was done under utmost secrecy and before the actual bombing on 6 August 1945, no more than a handful of people knew about it. Although more than 10,000 people were involved in the entire project, most worked as moles in the dark not knowing what was exactly happening out there. The scientists involved with the project were asked not to publish research papers related to nuclear research and military-related research in professional science magazines. Secrecy was necessary because the Allies didn't want to alert other countries, lest they accelerate their own nuclear research programmes. Despite such a large facility and a huge workforce, the Americans managed to keep the project under wraps, therefore managing to surprise Japan and the rest of the world with the devastating power of this wonder weapon.

Project Ultra: Breaking the Code

The importance of signal intelligence became evident during the two world wars. Intercepting enemy radio links provided very useful tactical as well as strategic information. To deny information to the enemy, various encrypting techniques were evolved. Before transmitting a message, it was encoded and at the destination, it had to be decoded using the same method that was applied during encryption. There was a constant endeavour by all defense establishments to have better and more sophisticated methods to keep an edge over the others.

Machine cipher was the biggest breakthrough technology in the field of encryption. Germany created Enigma, which they thought would encrypt communications that would be impenetrable by the Allies, and used it for all their communications. However, the British managed to break this code with the help of top minds who worked secretly at Bletchley Park, Buckinghamshire, a remote location in England. The Allies therefore had an edge over the Germans, as they were able to intercept and decipher every communication regarding their plans, intentions and strategy.

As General Harold Alexander of the British army put it,

'The knowledge not only of the enemy's precise strength and disposition, but also how, when and where he intends to carry out his operations brought a new dimension to the prosecution of the war.'[13] It is believed that the 'Ultra intelligence' provided by the boys at Bletchley shortened the war by two to four years. This technological achievement was indeed a game changer.

The Race for Space

Though the Americans had a definite head start over the Soviets in the field of nuclear weapons at the beginning of the Cold War, the Soviets outwitted them in the race for space. On 4 October 1957, they launched a less-than-2-feet-in-diameter artificial satellite, Sputnik, into space, which triggered the Space Race. The next level was to design and deploy intercontinental ballistic missiles, with both America and the USSR running neck-to-neck to maintain superiority during this time.

Stealth Technology

Radars gave the armed forces a virtual eye to locate aircraft flying in the vicinity. These became part of an early warning defense system that could alert a ground station about an approaching aircraft. Stealth technology was hence developed to avoid detection by enemy radars. They cover a range of technologies and techniques that make an aircraft, a submarine, a ship, or a missile less visible to enemy radars.

Americans were the first to research, develop and deploy stealth technology. They relied on the shape of the aircraft to reduce the radar cross-section and use of reflective surface material that would absorb radar waves rather than reflect

---

[13]Luck, K. (2008). *Fight*. WaterBrook.

them. The Russians later claimed to have come up with plasma technology, which would create a plasma shield around the aircraft to absorb radar waves.

The Element of Surprise in Business and Life

Surprise can be effectively used in business, especially in marketing. Instead of augmenting one's efforts, one should focus on sharpening one's strategy. Therefore, smarter the strategy, the lesser the efforts of the workforce in the marketplace.

Indirect or Flanking Attack

An indirect or flanking attack is an effective way of taking on an established rival brand. As per this, you can attack in an area where the market leader has not yet established their presence. One can do this either according to a geographical area where the rival brand is not strong enough or take a product approach and launch a product in a new category that does not compete directly with the rival product. It is very important to maintain the element of surprise so that the rival brand does not get time to react and use his massive resources to counter your move. To maintain secrecy, the entire operation should be undertaken clandestinely and the movement of marketing teams, surveys and test marketing must be conducted carefully and to a very limited extent.

Guerilla Tactics

When you are relatively too small to take on a flanking attack on the rival brand, it is better to use guerilla tactics, whereby you operate with stealth and choose a very small territory. The scope could be limited demographically or geographically. Guerilla tactics depend on good intelligence regarding enemy strengths, weaknesses, distribution systems, etc. It also relies on strong local support, which can be secretly built over a period of time. A guerilla fighter knows that the local population, if influenced, can provide resources like food, shelter and water. In business terms, this implies cultivating resources, people and groups to support your brand. Even local political patronage can be of great help. The timing in Guerilla warfare is very important; hit the enemy when he least expects it.

Price War

Price wars have been witnessed in almost every field of business. Telecom operators have resorted to price reductions across the world to lure customers from other operators and hold on to their existing customer base. Here again, surprise and speed matter. The marketing paradigm has yet again changed with the entry of e-commerce. Companies are announcing deals on a daily basis and a smart customer who can think on his feet has the last laugh.

Pricing comparisons are now possible with several websites specializing in getting you the best deals. It is difficult to get an advantage if the marketing strategists don't resort to 'reactive pricing,' where they change the price of a product almost in real time.

Instead of changing the price, companies can also launch a 'buy one, get one free' scheme.

There are hundreds of ways one can do trade promotions in a technology-intensive business battle scenario. Bundling of services, instalment schemes and loan tie-ups are some of the most used methods. Businesses are launching new schemes every day. Hence, surprise and deception play an important part, as merely stealth may not be of any significance in such a rapidly dynamic scenario.

Coming up with something new is inherent to human nature—change being the only constant. Since the last couple of centuries, business had been driven largely by technology. At the same time, technology has been reinventing itself. We started with gramophone records, which were soon replaced by magnetic tape spools and then tape cartridges. Then CDs were launched, which were replaced by pen drives within a couple of decades. This directly affected people in the business of music, films as well as data. Those who upgraded quickly thrived and those who didn't, struggled for survival or perished.

The Internet has been the biggest game changer in recent years. Riding on this communication juggernaut were cutting edge applications like email, Facebook, LinkedIn and Twitter. These were the killer apps. In the software and communication technology race, everyone is looking for the next killer app or a 'technological shocker' that will create the next big wave. While being a part of the technology race, one has to constantly keep an eye on the rear-view mirror to watch which technology will come up.

Quantum computers may be the next revolution in computing. These machines will be able to solve problems that conventional computers will take centuries to crack, thus helping in cryptology, artificial intelligence, forecasting, finance and medicine.

New ways of saving and producing energy and alternate fuel will also be a game changer. Substantial research is underway and the world has to find an alternative to fossil fuel, which has a limited lifespan. Fuel-efficient bulbs and LED lights are examples.

People crave the unexpected, and surprise can be used in a positive way in business. It's not expensive to achieve surprise. I remember during childhood, a brand of toothpaste used to have a 'golden charm' tucked inside the box carrying the tube. There were almost a hundred different little charms and as kids, we used to eagerly wait for one toothpaste to finish so that we could buy a new one to see what golden charm was hidden inside for us. The cost of the charm would have been ridiculously low, but the thrill was high, which made the brand popular and pushed up sales too. This is the best way to combine happiness with surprise, resulting in customer delight.

In personal affairs too, it is best to keep your cards close to your chest. Don't announce your intent to the world beforehand; sometimes a bit of secrecy can do a lot of good. To quote Carl Von Clausewitz, 'The backbone of surprise is fusing speed with secrecy.'

8

Credible Deterrence: How to Avoid a Conflict

> *'The supreme art of war is to subdue the enemy without fighting.'*
>
> —Sun Tzu

The Concept of Deterrence

Deterrence Theory was born at the beginning of the Cold War and therefore developed in a climate of uncertainty and great urgency. As a military strategy, 'deterrence' became a way of keeping the world safe after the Second World War. The US had amply demonstrated the destructive power of nuclear weapons when they bombed Hiroshima and Nagasaki on 6 and 9 August 1945 respectively, killing more than 129,000 people. The horrors of a nuclear holocaust became evident and no one wanted nuclear weapons to be ever used in the future. By then, the world was dominated politically as well as militarily by two superpowers—the US and the USSR. The world order was aligned into two blocs, one led by the Americans and the other by the Soviets, popularly known as the Western and the Eastern Bloc respectively.

In the late 1940s and 50s, a wide-ranging group of scholars—economists, political researchers and historians—based in American universities, sought to understand how best to utilize the new power of nuclear weapons to deter Soviet aggression against the US and its allies. In 1946, diplomat George Kennan explained this policy, 'The Soviet Union was a political force committed fanatically to the belief that with the US there can be no permanent modus vivendi [agreement between parties that disagree], as a result America's only choice was the long-term, patient but firm and vigilant containment of Russian expansive tendencies.'[14] The US and a few European countries formed the North Atlantic Treaty Organization (NATO) to coordinate defense mechanism against any Soviet invasion. In response to NATO, the Eastern Bloc created the Warsaw Pact to protect certain East European countries from any invasion by the Western Bloc.

This was the beginning of the Cold War between the only nuclear powers at that time. The term 'Cold War' first appeared in a 1945 essay written by the English writer George Orwell and the essay was named 'You and the Atomic Bomb'. It was termed as 'cold' because there were no major wars during this period between the two blocs, though there were several regional conflicts in Vietnam, Korea and the Gulf region.

The world went through the Cold War from 1947 to 1991. The Soviets and the Americans had profound political, ideological as well as economic differences. While America believed in democracy and a free economy, the Soviets were a single-party Marxist-Leninist communist state where the state controlled the economy. During this entire period, the world order was primarily bipolar.

During this time, both countries realized that there was a

---

[14]Rahim, A.K. (1990). George Frost Kennan: From Cold Warrior to Cold War Iconoclast, 1940-1950. *Pakistan Horizon*, 43(4), 73-95.

need to have an effective and workable deterrence in place to avoid a nuclear holocaust that could have been started by any one of the two powers. Since both had a huge nuclear arsenal and accurate delivery systems, the idea behind the deterrent system was to survive a surprise attack by the opponent without being totally annihilated or decimated. The strategy provided the rationale for an unprecedented arms buildup in the US. In 1950, a National Security Council report known as NSC-68 depicted that the country uses military force to 'contain' communist expansionism anywhere it seemed to be occurring. To that effect, the report stated a four-time escalation in the defense spending. Americans encouraged the development of arms, like the ones that have ended the Second World War.

While the world was standing at the brink of a nuclear holocaust, both superpowers, between them, were spending more than $50 million a day on nuclear weapons at one point of time, dubbed as the Arms Race. A nuclear war would not only kill millions instantaneously, but would lead to a nuclear winter, which could last for decades or even centuries. This could result in every human on the earth to die of cold and starvation.

The concept of deterrence can thus be defined as the 'use of credible threat by one country to convince the other country to refrain from taking any course of action or act of aggression against it.'[15] Bernard Brodie, an American military strategist, wrote, 'A credible nuclear deterrent must be always at the ready, but never used.'[16]

---

[15]Huth, P.K. (1999). "Deterrence and International Conflict: Empirical Findings and Theoretical Debate", *Annual Review of Political Science*, 2: 25–48, doi:10.1146/annurev.polisci.2.1.25

[16]Brodie, B. (1959), "8", *The Anatomy of Deterrence" as found in Strategy in the*

The credibility of a nuclear threat is established by a nation state when it amply demonstrates that it has the nuclear capability and in case required, will use it for its own protection. As an analogy, it is like two men who hate each other, but would still like to avoid a fight. Each one is carrying a fully loaded pistol for his defense and tells the other that the pistol is loaded and he would not hesitate to use it in case the other party draws the gun first. This is a signal for 'back off or else'. Here, the loaded pistol and the clarity of intent to use it deters the other party to even draw the gun, leave aside using it against the foe.

In international relations, the deterrent policy implies threat of military retaliation with nuclear weapons by the political leadership of one state to the leadership of another to prevent the other state from resorting to use of military force in pursuit of its aggressive or expansionist foreign policy. The central idea is to avoid a major conflict. Deterrence, therefore, aims to say that military strategy can no longer be viewed as a strategy for absolute victory. With this strategy in place, the Americans ensured that any attempt by the Soviets to capture Western Europe would become a protracted and fierce conventional military battle.

Multipolar Scenario

After the disintegration of the USSR by 1991, the world order changed to unipolar as the US was the only power that had a huge military might, economic power, technological prowess and a massive nuclear arsenal.

However, other nations also steadily developed nuclear

Missile Age, Princeton: Princeton University Press, pp. 264–304 weapons and the balance of power shifted once again from unipolar to multipolar as China, the UK, France, India, Pakistan, Israel and North Korea joined the nuclear club. Today, therefore, the world order has become more complex and some strategists argue that such a state of affairs makes the world unsafe as compared to the earlier situation where there were only two decision-making points.

Credible Deterrence

When the cost of aggression or attack exceeds the expected benefit, the adversary will not attack and the deterrence will work. For deterrence to work, the adversary should be *made to believe* or get *convinced* that engaging in aggression *will not be worth it*. The concept of deterrence focuses on the number of survivable weapons necessary to threaten a select set of enemy targets whether urban/industrial, military, political centres or other physical assets. Possessing the forces necessary to threaten the selected targets essentially is equated to having a credible and reliable deterrent. During the Cold War, it was easy for the Americans to deter an attack on their homeland by the Soviet Union. Due to the overwhelming distance, the Soviets could not have launched a successful conventional invasion on American soil. Such deterrence is termed as 'deterrence by denial'. In case of a nuclear attack by the Soviets, America was in a position to respond with a devastating nuclear strike on the Soviet homeland. This was a credible threat because such an attack would have caused unprecedented damage to them.

In Western Europe, the scenario was different. The European conventional war machinery was considered inferior to the Soviets. Therefore, providing deterrence to Western Europe was not that simple for the US. Americans ensured that sufficient force was deployed in Western Europe so that it would not be an easy victory for the Soviets in case of a conventional war. Yet, this was not a sufficient deterrent for the Soviets not to venture on an all-out attack on Western Europe.

The US projected to the Soviets that in case they resorted to conventional invasion, America would strike the Soviet homeland with nuclear weapons. This was not a credible threat, as the Soviets knew that Americans would never use nuclear weapons to protect Western Europe. To deal with this ambiguity and uncertainty, the Americans decided to deploy tactical nuclear weapons in Western Europe, which were capable of striking the conventional Soviet forces without having to hit USSR directly. This was known as 'extended deterrence' during the Cold War.

The current Indo-Pak scenario and the strained relations between the two countries is again very complex. Both are nuclear states and have large, conventional war machines. To avoid a conventional war, which will be very costly for Pakistan, it has been resorting to terrorist attacks across the border. The cost of such terrorist activities is very low in terms of manpower and equipment. Therefore, even if some of these fail at the hands of Indian security forces, it does not become a deterrent for them. Despite concerted efforts by Indian security forces, the success rate of terrorist attacks is high. For India, it is thus impossible to achieve deterrence by denial. On the other hand, achieving deterrence by punishment is very difficult as the terrorists pose as non-state actors and therefore there is no homeland that India can technically hit at. Attacking terrorist camps in Pakistan-occupied Kashmir or limited strikes across the borders will not deter Pakistan from resorting to terrorist attacks. For them, this is a low-cost, high-yield strategy to keep India on its toes.

Minimum Credible Deterrence

To avoid creating an unnecessarily large nuclear stockpile, the concept of minimum or minimal credible deterrence was evolved. It can be devised that it is only when the state feels threatened that it opts to defend its territory and sovereignty, which compels it to maximize and enrich its security measures. However, in order to maintain a deterrent posture, the number of weapons is not necessary, as the possession of nuclear weapons itself is enough. Even if a state posseses a single nuclear weapon, it is sufficient to discourage the nuclear aggression of the other state. Therefore, minimum credible deterrence is completely different from nuclear supremacy and nuclear parity. It also assumes 'no first use,' underlining that the only purpose of possessing nuclear weapons is to deter an adversary by making the cost of his first strike unacceptably high. To make it credible, the intent is made very clear that any nuclear attack would be responded to adequately by a retaliatory nuclear strike. This way, a nuclear state doesn't have to invest heavily into keeping a large stockpile, while still ensuring that it is secured from a nuclear attack. Therefore, instead of having a large counter-force, the state favours a survivable force that can retaliate to deliver a sufficiently hard counter-blow to the adversary, hence keeping the deterrent factor intact.

In practice, both the Americans and the Soviets got into a fierce arms race during the Cold War and developed very robust first strike and second strike capabilities. They, in a way, had more nuclear weapons than required to ensure their safety. On the other hand, China decided to have only that much nuclear stockpile that was sufficient to deter an adversary by destroying its key strategic locations. Similarly, India and Pakistan both also adopted a policy of minimum credible deterrence.

The advantage of minimum credible deterrence is that it squarely addresses the security issue of a nation state without getting into an arms race. While not increasing the number of weapons, a nation may decide to keep investing in advanced weapons to keep its credibility intact. States that follow the policy of minimum credible deterrence are able to carry out arms reduction during arms negotiations without becoming vulnerable to nuclear threats by adversaries.

National security policies and military strategies have indoctrinated the theory of Mutual Assured Destruction (MAD). In this theory, a full-scale use of high-yield, mass destruction weapons by opposing parties would result in the complete and irrevocable annihilation of both attacker and defender.

At the beginning of the Cold War, Americans had an edge over the Soviets in terms of nuclear weapon capability. Therefore, they felt very safe that the latter would never launch a nuclear strike against them. Gradually, the Soviets achieved nuclear parity with them and this was a great cause of concern for the Americans. The Cold War entered a dangerous and unmanageable phase, taking the conflict to levels that Americans had never faced before.

In the wake of a war with the USSR, the US lost the advantage of a superior economy, better alliances and a sound decision-making system. By then, both nation states had enough nuclear stockpile to destroy each other many times over. The advantage of a preemptive first strike to annihilate the adversary totally was no more a viable military strategy as both of them were capable of inflicting a devastating blow after having absorbed a first strike. Therefore, whosoever started the fight would also be wiped out. MAD was thus officially accepted as a military doctrine by both.

To make MAD look credible, both the Americans and the Soviets invested heavily in their nuclear arsenal. They both diversified their nuclear delivery systems, like nuclear bomber aircraft, and submarine-launched and intercontinental ballistic missiles hidden in missile silos in top-secret locations. Since it was a three-branched nuclear capability, it was referred to as the 'Nuclear Triad'. This escalated the tensions, and though both lived in fear of each other, the world was safe from a nuclear holocaust.

Arms control efforts thereafter have been to find a minimum level of assured destruction. The Strategic Arms Limitation Treaty and the Strategic Arms Reduction Treaty are efforts to stabilize mutual deterrence. Richard Nixon and Leonid Brezhnev signed the former in 1972, while George Bush and Soviet Premier Mikhail Gorbachev signed the latter in 1991. Besides limiting the strategic offensive nuclear weapons, both powers agreed to ban anti-ballistic missile (ABM) systems as well. Each side was permitted to have only two ABM sites—one protecting the capital and the other, a long-range missile site.

Exerting Influence at the Global Scale

Because the central idea of nuclear deterrence is to avoid war, it does not let a nation state influence the rest of the world. A powerful nation can exert influence on a global or international scale only by its ability to project its power through conventional military might. The British were the first to use the Royal Navy to make their presence felt across the world in the 19th century. They wanted to expand their empire by establishing colonies yet avoiding direct conflict with other nations.

The US Department of Defense defines power projection as the 'ability of a nation to apply all or some of its elements of national power—political, economic, informational or military—to rapidly and effectively deploy and sustain forces in and from multiple dispersed locations to respond to crises, to contribute to deterrence, and to enhance regional stability'. It is pertinent to mention that possessing formidable conventional war machines also contributes to deterrence, as others who do not possess a matching war-waging capability will not dare to venture against such a military power. While long-range ballistic missiles and aircraft can deliver severe punishment to any adversary located at a distance, it is important for a nation to be able to deploy its military might, including men and material, rapidly across any region where it wants to wield its influence. The ability to conduct and coordinate joint operations integrating land forces, the air force and the navy is at the heart of power projection. Since the Cold War, the Americans have constantly flexed their muscles and ensured their presence globally.

Examples Where Nuclear Deterrence Prevented a Major War

The Berlin Blockade (1948)

The Berlin Blockade was an attempt in 1948 by the Soviet Union to restrict the ability of France, Great Britain and the US to travel to their zones of Berlin, which lay within USSR-occupied East Germany. After the Second World War, Germany had been divided into two parts—the eastern portion went to the USSR, and the Americans and their allies had the control of the western part.

A major crisis precipitated between the Soviets and the Americans in April 1948. The former decided to block the western allies' access to railways and roads, to protest against the introduction of new currency by the latter, who retaliated by airlifting supplies to the people of West Germany. Over 321 days, the US and its allies made more than 200,000 flights into West Berlin to provide necessities to the people living in that sector. The effort achieved widespread public support and on 12 May 1949, the Soviets, concluding that the blockade had failed, reopened the borders. East and West Germany were established as separate republics later that month.

President Harry S. Truman also deployed B-29 Bombers to the UK in order to apply pressure on the Soviets. They were presumed to be nuclear-capable and this information was leaked to the press. This was the first time that a nuclear threat was used during the Cold War. It worked in the favour of the Western Bloc and the crisis ended peacefully. In this case, it was a combination of conventional war-waging capability displayed by massive airlift capability and nuclear power diplomacy, which achieved the desired result.

The Cuban Crisis (1962)

In October 1962, the Soviets and Americans came very close to triggering a nuclear war. This was dubbed as the Cuban Missile Crisis, which lasted for just 13 days, but had put both countries on full military and diplomatic alert. During this crisis, the leaders of America and the Soviet Union engaged in a political and military standoff in October 1962, over the installation of nuclear armed Soviet missiles on Cuba, just about 90 km from US shores.

The Americans had their nuclear ballistic missiles in Italy and Turkey, which were a direct threat to the USSR. Americans also attempted a military invasion of Cuba to overthrow the communist government under Fidel Castro. This failed operation was named the 'Bay of Pigs Invasion' and apparently created fear amongst the Cuban political leadership of a direct American intervention into their homeland.

In response to this situation, and to keep the US in check, Soviet Premier Nikita Khrushchev agreed to the request by Cuba to deploy nuclear missiles on its soil, which would prevent America from interfering in their internal affairs. The deployed missiles were less than 100 miles from Florida and this got the Americans literally rattled.

Both countries were trying to exert pressure on each other, militarily as well as diplomatically. Americans were ready to go for an airstrike either to destroy the Soviet missile bases in Cuba or have a naval blockade of Cuba. The direct involvement of President John F. Kennedy and Premier Khrushchev was enough to indicate the seriousness of the matter. After a number of serious diplomatic efforts, the countries agreed to finally come to a consensus. The Americans withdrew their missiles deployed in Europe, and the Soviet removed theirs from Cuba. The world was at the brink of a nuclear war, which was averted through a constant dialogue between the two heads of state. Both were thus sobered by the Cuban Missile Crisis. The following year, a direct 'hotline' communication link was installed between Washington D.C. and Moscow to help diffuse similar situations. The two superpowers signed two treaties related to nuclear weapons as well.

Brinkmanship

An open question in nuclear deterrence theory is whether and how the balance of military power affects the dynamics of escalation. The idea of brinkmanship is to push a dangerously confrontational situation to the edge of disaster so as to gain maximum advantage by the end of the event. It is a test of nerves, an understanding of the situation and a correct assessment of 'how far is too far?' for both the parties. This could happen in politics, international relations, labour relations, military operations, business and strategy, and is now prevalent in many high-stake litigation and coalition government formations and business deals as well.

Deterrance acquired a very prominent place during the Cold War, when the US and the USSR had achieved nuclear parity and were armed to the teeth, ready to go for each other. The balance of conventional power between the NATO and Warsaw Pact was not vital, as deterrence depended on the 'balance of resolve'. The balance of power between the countries was unimportant considering those states occupied large nuclear arsenals. The threat of nuclear force was used to escalate a crisis—pushing the opponent to a point to allow the desired concessions. The Berlin Blockade and Cuban Missile Crisis demonstrate this strategy. This word 'brinkmanship' was coined by Adlai Ewing Stevenson, an American politician and a diplomat during the Kennedy and Johnson administration.

For a threat to be effective, it has to appear credible and should be continuously escalated. This is a dangerous ploy and therefore the 'push' needs to be carefully managed. If you look at a glass full of water with a little space for accommodating more water, you need to pour that extra bit very carefully. Once it reaches the brink, you need to stop, else water will flow out and there is no way to reverse the situation. The most difficult part of this strategy is to convince the other party regarding one's own commitment and intention to carry out the threat.

There is always a danger where the events may have a snowball effect, triggering a disaster. In a cat and mouse chase, a small human misjudgement can trigger a nuclear attack, resulting in a full-blown nuclear war. On 27 October 1962, during the Cuban Missile Crisis, several US Navy destroyers along with an aircraft carrier located a diesel-powered Soviet submarine near Cuban waters. In order to force it to surface, they began dropping depth charges. To avoid these, the Soviet submarine went deeper into the ocean and therefore, could neither communicate with their contacts back home nor monitor any radio links to assess the situation. The commander of the submarine did not know if the war between the US and the USSR had already started. This submarine was armed with a nuclear torpedo and Valentin Grigorievitch Savitsky, the captain of the ship, believing that the war had started, wanted to use the nuclear weapon under his command. As per protocol, he, along with his second in command and a political officer on board, had to unanimously agree in order to fire the nuclear weapon. Better sense prevailed on the second-in-command captain Arkhipov, who did not agree with the option of using a nuclear weapon. The fatigued captain could have well started a nuclear war, culminating into a major catastrophe. In 2002, while discussing the Cuban Crisis, Robert McNamara who was the US secretary of state during the crisis said, 'We came very close to a nuclear war, closer than we knew at that time.'

The Madman Theory

Deterrence is all about perception, which can be created by several means. One of them is to show that the person in command is a bit edgy or irrational and hence a little provocation could trigger a volatile reaction.

This is what US President Richard Nixon did. He asked his administration to get the Soviets to believe that he was a madman. The Soviets were therefore made to believe that a little provocation from them could make him take an irrational decision, which could well be a nuclear strike! It worked in the favour of Americans during the Nixon regime. This came to be known as the Madman Theory in the American foreign policy framework.

Why and How Does Deterrence Work?

Whether it is a nation state, a business corporation or a group of people, ultimately it is the core group within, which controls the actions and reactions of the conglomeration. The act of deterrence, therefore, is directed towards such people. In many cases, it is one man or woman at the top who takes a call for a reaction, a response or an action in a given scenario.

Criminal law, which deals with individuals as well as organizations, has deterrence at its very core. It is one of the objectives of law that members of a society should be dissuaded or discouraged, so as not to commit or repeat a criminal activity. Since criminal justice policies are based on the deterrence philosophy, debates on the deterrence effect of punishment continue to be addressed in criminological research programmes. 'Boot camps' for teenage offenders and 'scared straight' programmes continue to rely on the deterrence theory. In their effort to have more empirical support, criminologists are working towards the direction of expanding deterrence concepts from celerity and severity, to accommodate more informal social procedures of reward and ethical beliefs. Criminal law presupposes that the criminal reasonably reflects upon the consequences of committing a crime. Acts of crime that are triggered and committed in the heat of the moment cannot be prevented by a criminal system based on deterrence.

Legal deterrence works because a person is afraid of the consequences of being caught and/or due to a deep sense of moral values. Yet there are rogues with criminal minds who don't care for values and are bold enough not to worry about the consequences of the crime they are about to commit. If there are rouges amongst people, then there can be rogue states too. After all, people who can well be rogues may run such states. For deterrence at the international level, it is assumed that the people who are at the helm of affairs and are decision-makers have good control over their emotions and actions. They are also capable of applying their minds and making choices based on logic and the larger interest, and not on passion and emotions.

More Forms of Deterrence

Geographical Deterrence

Some natural obstacles or climatic conditions by themselves can become a deterrent.

- **The Russian Winter:** In 1812, Napoleon was defeated in Russia because he lost almost half his army to the Russian winter. His soldiers died of cold and disease and he had to face a humiliating retreat. Something similar happened to the German armies that ventured to attack Russia in 1941, a little before the Russian winter set in. Hitler was expecting a quick victory and was totally unprepared for the severe weather. The Germans lost almost a quarter of its force in the first few months because of the extreme cold.

- **The Mighty Himalayas:** Thick snow and insurmountable heights have made the Himalayas formidable natural obstacles for those who have wanted to launch an attack on Indian soil. These mountain ranges extend from the east to the west and provide a gigantic 2,500 km wall protecting the Indian subcontinent from external aggression. With depth ranging between 250 and 320 km, it is difficult to even maintain roads, thus making it a logistical nightmare for any potential adversary to attack India.
- **The English Channel:** The English Channel separates England from the rest of Europe. It is 650 km long and its width varies between 30 and 240 km. During the Second World War, this waterbody became a formidable natural barrier for the Germans, who were able to capture almost the entire Europe including France at lightning speed. It similarly posed a big problem for the British and Allied forces when they wanted to launch a counter-offensive on the Germans to dislodge them from France and other occupied European nations. They had to rely on a huge naval power and a large number of troops to do so.

Man-Made Obstacles

Obstacles have been created throughout the history of warfare to deter adversaries from getting a free run over a territory.

- **The Great Wall of China:** This wall, which dates back to the 7th century, is probably the largest and the longest man-made obstacle ever created. It runs east to west across the northern borders of China and was built to protect the Chinese states and kingdoms from invasion by nomadic groups and foreign adversaries. It is an 8,800 km-long formidable obstacle made of bricks, stone, wood and mud, and was built in different phases with more than 25,000 watchtowers around 20 ft wide and 20 to 25 ft high.
- **Forts and Castles:** Forts and castles are generally built on high ground to deny easy access to the adversary. This also gives the strategic advantage of being on a vantage point, which commands better visibility.
- **Pacts and Treatise:** Political pacts and treatises have been historically executed by nation states to maintain a balance of power and to protect their own national interest. Such treatises deter powerful belligerent states from attacking the weaker ones. In many cases, they are executed to achieve short-term gains. Pacts and treaties are simply defined as 'written agreements signed by official representatives of two independent states, that include promises to assist a partner in the event of military conflict, to remain neutral at the wake of war, to refrain from military conflict with each other or to consult and cooperate during international crisis which may contain potential for military conflict.'

Just before the Second World War started, Europe was going through a political upheaval and an environment of total distrust prevailed amongst most European nations. The European powers that had military and economic might were England, France, Germany, Italy and the USSR. After the First World War, the Treaty of Versailles put Germans in a very disadvantageous position. They were not satisfied with what was meted out to them by the rest of the European allies. Germany under Adolf Hitler was pacing ahead as a power to reckon with and was demonstrating its resolve to 'fight it out' for its own rights. The British, French and Soviets wanted to have a military pact to contain Hitler's expansionist plans. At the same time, the Soviets were also secretly engaged by the Germans to negotiate a treaty with them, offering them a better deal than the British and the French. Germany was keen to have a pact signed with the USSR, because if war broke out, Germany would require raw material from them. A non-aggression pact would also allow Germany to go the whole hog, attacking the rest of Europe without worrying about Soviet intervention.

Though tripartite negotiations had started between the Soviets, the British and the French in May–June 1939, Germany managed to quickly turn the tables and negotiated a pact with the USSR on 23 August 1939. This was known as the Molotov–Ribbentrop Pact. Within a few days of this pact, Germany started its invasion of Europe by attacking Poland, and in a lightning war, managed to capture a considerable portion of Europe. Germany, therefore, managed to achieve some quick victories in the continent. The Molotov Ribbentrop Pact had served its purpose and once it was no longer required, Hitler broke it by invading the USSR on 22 June 1941.

Deterrence in Personal Affairs

Individuals take certain measures to protect themselves from criminals, thieves and thugs, which act like a deterrence. For instance, one can keep a dog at home for one's own safety. The dog becomes a 'deterrence'. To ensure that thieves and thugs *know* you have a dog at home, you put a big signboard outside your home saying 'Beware of the dog' and put a picture of a Doberman. This becomes 'credible deterrence'. You need not keep ten dogs when one would suffice, and that becomes a 'minimum credible deterrence'.

In the same way, shops and departmental stores instal CCTV cameras for surveillance to protect themselves from shoplifters. However, once they put up a signboard saying 'This store is under surveillance,' it becomes more credible. The idea is to avoid shoplifting and not to catch a thief after he has stolen your stuff.

Using Deterrence to Protect Business Affairs

Today technology and globalization have opened up business avenues for individuals and corporations that were not available to them a couple of decades ago. As a result, many more are entering the business arena. This has resulted in fierce cut-throat competition and an environment where every business organization, big or small, feels threatened.

Survival depends on being able to understand the competitive environment and being able to assess the ability and intentions of your competition to 'hurt you'.

The capability of your competitor to attack you depends upon his experience in the field, credibility and ability to invest, absorb losses and take risks. In other words, you need to assess his ability to sustain the business over a reasonable period, which might be longer than your own ability to hold out.

The financial strength of the opponent is one of the most important parameters that need to be scrutinized. Opponents with deep pockets can bring in deep trouble. A strong, top management with a reputation is again a strong point that cannot be ignored. In certain areas, manpower plays a pivotal role. For instance, in higher education, the teaching faculty matters the most. You cannot easily browbeat a college that has a well-qualified and experienced teaching staff. In certain businesses, a strong marketing team can make all the difference and can be a deterrent for the competition.

It is also important to understand the credibility of this threat. A competitor's credibility stems from his propensity or disposition to get into this business and his inclination to go all the way. You also need to consider the history of your competitor—is he aggressive, bold, decisive and above all, enterprising? Does he play by the rules or is a master in unethical business practices? It also depends on whether your competitor takes you as a credible threat.

Aggressive business campaigns that attack another brand or product are often a result of how one perceives the stand of the opponent's action. Certain organizations are more reactive in nature. In most cases, the proactive nature is a natural tendency to wait and watch before making any major move.

The business environment is very complex as commerce flows across national boundaries. Though laws try to provide a level playing field for everyone, some win and some lose. A lot depends on how one strategizes to make the best of what can be done within the rules of the game. Business interests and national interests are both handled by people who are at the helm of affairs. Therefore, a lot depends on the intent and the credibility of the people who take such decisions.

9

Mobilization: Building and Maintaining Resources

> *'I am tempted to make a slightly exaggerated statement: that logistics is all of war-making, except shooting the guns, releasing the bombs, and firing the torpedoes.'*
> —Admiral Lynde D. McCormick, US Navy

Introduction

The word 'mobilization' means to assemble or coordinate for a purpose or as if for war. It is a highly potent motivating and invigorating expression. Mobilization is the essence and lifeblood of the armed forces across the world, without which no military operation can ever be conceived or launched.

The very basic and essential requirement for an operation is to muster men and material. Every organized body of men in uniform has to meet this pertinent criterion of resource mobilization, and due to this, they take pride in being self-contained at all levels. From the smallest formation, a platoon consisting of 36 men, to a company of about 120–150 and a battalion of close to 700 men, this principle of remaining self-sufficient is sacrosanct across the board. Every unit or sub-unit must be able to support itself in all respects.

What All Does Mobilization Entail?

For an army to go to war, a nation has to stand behind it with all its might. A fighting force needs resources that include vehicles, food supplies, medical equipment and medicines, communication equipment, clothing, shelters and tents besides arms and ammunition, which may be manufactured internally or imported. In a long-drawn war, an army needs to replenish materials as well as manpower because of casualties.

The first and most difficult part of mobilization requires creating resources—men and material, both. An army can have a grand mobilization plan, but will not be able to do much unless and until it gets what it needs. Most contemporary wars have amply demonstrated that the manufacturing and production of military hardware was essential to win a war. When America joined the First World War in 1917, without sufficient war hardware as well as the inability to produce it, it created a crippling situation for itself. The American armed forces had no clue either about the quantum of the war, or the timelines involved. The civil administration was not even fully aware of the nation's industrial capacity. America realized that mobilization of material was costly as well as complex. They also understood that industrial capacity cannot be created overnight.

After the First World War, Americans put in a concerted effort to augment its manufacturing base during peacetime. For the first time, they realized that the entire national economy must get involved for a modern war that demands massive mechanized forces and sophisticated weapons. An army industrial college was established and for the next two decades, America created a strong backbone for its armed forces.

Before the Second World War, Americans, who were so far away from Europe, were not keen to get involved in any war. They were not interested in participating in world affairs and therefore adopted an isolationist policy. But as Italy, Japan and Germany expressed their desire to follow an expansionist approach, President Roosevelt initiated a limited preparedness initiative, instead of an all-out war effort. This time, America was better prepared. As soon as the Second World War started, the American Congress allocated large sums for war preparations. Beginning with half a billion dollars in 1939, it went up to $8 billion in 1940 and $26 billion in 1941. By the time the Pearl Harbour attack took place on 7 December 1941, Americans had considerable military investments in place. The expenditure on combat ammunition alone was swiftly notched up to $38 billion in 1943 and $42 billion in 1944. In comparison, the USSR spent $14 billion in 1943 and $16 billion in 1944. Germany invested $13.5 billion and $17 billion, and UK had put in $11 billion each.[17]

The biggest challenge for Americans was to move every bit of equipment and every man from their country to Europe. It would be pertinent to note that America became a superpower and still is, not because of its capability in cutting edge IT alone, but due to its huge industrial base. The US has the capacity to produce steel, cement, aircraft, weapons, clothing, dairy and agricultural produce in very large quantities.

The theory and doctrine of nuclear deterrence is based on

---

[17]Goldsmith, R. W. (1946). The Power of Victory: Munitions Output in World War II. *The Journal of Military History*, 10, 69.

the overwhelming ability of one nation being able to inflict unacceptable damage to its adversary to dissuade them from starting a nuclear war. The destruction of a large portion of industrial capability (rendering it incapable of mobilizing for war in the near future) is at the core of the unacceptability criterion.

During the Cold War, Robert McNamara, US secretary of defense, created a military doctrine called MAD, whose central theme was nuclear deterrence. Both the US and the USSR were capable of totally annihilating each other as they both possessed sufficient nuclear capabilities to do so and therefore, it was presumed that none of them would dare to start a war, thereby leading to deterrence. In this doctrine, the destruction of industrial capacity is also important to the strategy.

From 1962 to 1967, the US got entangled in the Vietnam War, which was again fought away from its own shores. Mobilization was yet again a challenge. Though America contributed to the Second World War immensely and also committed itself to Vietnam, their ability to apply their might was considerably diminished because of the distance in both these wars.

Economist Kenneth Boulding devised the 'Loss of Strength Gradient' (LSG), indicating that the amount of a country's military power that could be brought to bear in any part of the world depended on the geographical distance. LSG graphically depicted that the further away the target of interest, the less strength could be made available. LSG is the essence of logistical efforts, which comprises the second part of the mobilization effort. The further the place of action, the less effective is the war effort, and substantial efforts are required for the planning and execution of logistical operations. In the context of military operations, logistics entails planning, acquisition, distribution, storage, movement, maintenance and even the disposal and evacuation of men and material. It also means the evacuation and hospitalization of casualties and building or acquiring accommodation, roads and bridges wherever required.

Challenges in Military Mobilization

Though mobilization for military operations is more complex than any civilian project or operation; in certain situations, business projects also may get impacted due to similar problems. Mobilization during natural calamities in a civil setting will definitely face similar challenges.

- **Terrain**: Military operations can be conducted in different terrains by different formations of the same army. For instance, units of the Indian Army deployed in high-altitude snow-bound areas in the north have to deal with the mountains and jungles of the northeast. The western sector has plains and a desert with its own challenges. Requirements for equipment, clothing, food, shelter and even training is different for different terrains. Terrain also dictates the possible speed of movement and the mode of transportation. The intensity of difficulty depends on the nature of terrain as well. While planning mobilization, the type of terrain and its impact on the movement of troops and material have to be kept in mind.
- **Weather**: Snow, rain, heat and humidity affects men and material both. Weather dictates the speed and quantum of logistical support that is possible. Snow and rain, for instance, can create havoc for armies because they impede movement. Hence, it is critical to factor in

weather conditions beforehand.

- **Unexpected Requirements**: Throughout military history, there may have hardly been any military campaign that was executed 'exactly as planned.' Military operations—though planned very meticulously—make a number of assumptions about the enemy, as planners do not get very precise or authentic information regarding several parameters, and these parameters impact execution directly. Due to the inaccuracy of information, military commanders have to keep their options open to make mid-course correction or take another line of action that was not a part of the initial plan. This directly impacts the mobilization scheme and the planning staff has to respond to these changes in almost real time. Despite the best efforts, the best may not be made available to the force commander, who then has to be mentally agile to come up with on-the-spot improvization. Such unexpected situations can crop up at the tactical as well as strategic levels.
- **Operating in Enemy Territory**: There are challenges in resource mobilization in an enemy area that has been won over by friendly forces. Since it is an unfamiliar area, the planning is usually done based on maps, the information available through military intelligence and very recently, through satellite imaging. Mobilizing resources in an alien area could spring several surprises for the planners. However, if the enemy towns can be captured intact, considerable enemy resources can be gainfully utilized. Roads, bridges, warehouses, hospitals, accommodation, food, water and communications are some of the prized possessions for the troops that move in. Many times, this is factored into the mobilization scheme, and if everything

goes as per plans, the occupying forces can manage to survive on the war booty.

- **Enemy Action:** In a war-like scenario, movement even in your own territory may not be free. The enemy will always target your ships, convoys, aircraft and railways with any means available. They will ensure that your supplies are cut off so that your forces become ineffective. During war, most military convoys, therefore, need to move with adequate protection. For instance, ships carrying military supplies are accompanied by war ships, and supply-carrying aircraft have fighter aircraft giving them protection from enemy aircraft.

- **Lack of Full and Authentic Information:** Before any military operation is launched, a major intelligence-gathering exercise is usually conducted. Basis this intelligence, the course of action is decided. Multiple sources of intelligence are available to a fighting force, yet the picture is seldom complete. Many times due to the misleading counter-intelligence efforts of the enemy, the available information is either spurious or not authentic. Therefore, planning the mobilization of men and material is never without risk, and this needs to be factored into the mobilization plan. In the Second World War, several times both the Axis powers as well as the Allies were duped by each other regarding the movement of troops and supply-carrying convoys.

- **Moving Under Stealth**: Mobilization has to be conducted under stealth and secrecy, because of the fear of an attack and the vulnerability of one's troops. Timings and routes are well-guarded secrets. Many times in conventional warfare, troop movements by road and even railways are undertaken at night. To a large extent, this can take care of the problem, but may not totally protect the troops. In the industry and business scenario, new product launches have to be a closely guarded secret and hence, the transportation of such products to different locations is done in secrecy.

Maintaining Reserves

Every nation and its armed forces need to remain prepared to defend the country in case a war breaks out with its neighbours or in regions of interest. Fundamental to this preparedness is the availability of military hardware, food, medicine and fuel in sufficient quantities at multiple locations and within an acceptable timeframe. Planning to stock material in advance is done according to threat perception at the military as well as political levels. War reserve stocks are maintained in prepositioned locations and are to be used during the war as and when needed. As predicted by military planners, these locations are decided depending on the anticipated requirements. In addition to stocking ammunition, which is rapidly expendable in war, petroleum reserves are also considered as a strategic reserve.

Almost all army ordnance factories and R&D establishments are set up somewhat in the central part of the country so as to keep these resources safe from enemy action. As a basic principle of war, ammunition dumps are created at strategic locations well in advance, because these locations are not easily accessible and material takes a longer time to reach. Keeping this in mind, most armies operating in the mountains resort to 'winter stocking,' which implies that food, ammunition and fuel are all dumped during summers when the going is good and the roads are fully operational. In winter, such areas are inhospitable and many of the strategic areas are cut off for several months, especially when it snows heavily.

While in the military context, the stock points and quantity of stock that is positioned are located as per tactical and strategic plans (with little concern about costs), the forward stock locations in the civil environment are usually decided based on return on investment. Companies that are into maintenance and servicing need to have spare parts positioned in such a way as to minimize the cost of this exercise, while providing better service and minimizing down time. Transportation costs continue to increase, and therefore, having more stock points at appropriate locations has been accepted as an optimal solution for transportation efficiency in recent times.

General Staff (GS) reserve is yet another concept that the armed forces follow for critical, unpredictable needs. Those officers who assist field commanders in the planning and execution of operations in the battlefield constitute the GS. They are directly responsible for the conduct and outcome of military operations, and hence have a right over others. They are, in fact, an active part of the force as the battle unfolds and hence, in the position to know what is required, when and where. Therefore, certain critical stores and equipment could be kept earmarked, to be released only with the orders of the GS.

Normally, the approval for such a release is accorded at the highest level and under the most critical circumstances. Most armies of the world follow a very simple and yet effective way of dealing with the day-to-day running of the organization, in peacetime as well as war. They have three branches: i) the

G Branch, or the GS branch, which is responsible for operations and intelligence; ii) the AG Branch (Adjutant Generals Branch), which deals with all matters related to personnel management; and 3) the Q branch (Quarter Master Branch), which is responsible for logistics and equipment support.

The chief operating officer (COO) and his staff usually constitute the GS in a company; some may like to call it the core group. Depending on the type of business and operational unpredictability, some resources could be kept up the sleeve by the COO as a GS reserve, only to be released with his explicit approval. Here, the COO, who is the head of operations, is assured that he has a dedicated resource at his beck and call.

Inventory control in any industrial setup is an important aspect. Critical components for maintenance have to be kept at locations such that demands/requirements can be met at short notice. In case of manufacturing, adequate raw material should be available at different places to cater to demand fluctuations. Some of the demands are seasonal and hence, predictable. For instance, soft drink companies know that demand for its products will shoot up during summers. It must keep adequate supply of the raw material and bottles available in the plants so that seasonal demands can be responded to.

Military Operations Where Mobilization Was the Key

Throughout the history of warfare, especially in the last 100 years, there have been military campaigns where the outcomes largely depended on mobilization. Since mobilization is effected by terrain and weather, it will be good to look at operations conducted in different environments. It is also important to appreciate the gigantic effort and coordination required to conduct military operations.

Operation Barbarossa: Depth and Weather
(22 June–5 December 1941)

Operation Barbarossa was the biggest military operation in the history of warfare, and this invasion of the USSR by Nazi Germany finally led to the downfall of Hitler's regime and his ultimate defeat, leading to the end of the Second World War.

Hitler wanted to conquer the USSR and destroy communism, which would also give more 'lebensraum' for the German people. He also looked at the USSR as a breadbasket for Germany, especially the fertile farmlands of Ukraine. Having tasted a string of victories on the Western front, Hitler was confident of achieving his goal, though part of his military GS was not. Despite this, Hitler ordered his senior generals to hit the USSR with utmost brutality; it had to be savage, unmerciful and unprecedented.

With every country attacked by Germany until then falling apart like a pack of cards, they had every reason to expect victory. Hitler's staff had a couple of good reasons to believe that they could pull this off: in the late 1930s, Stalin had executed more than 50 per cent of his own military officers during purges, depleting their fighting capability; and Hitler had executed a non-aggression pact with the USSR in 1939, which gave the Soviets a false sense of security that Germany would never attack them, and definitely not before finishing the war with Britain. This faith made them lower their guard and the Germans were expecting to catch them with their pants down. However, German generals were aware that many invasions on the USSR had failed miserably in the past because of the vastness of the land and its cold weather. It was popularly said that the USSR had three generals: General

Winter, General Frost and General Snow.

By December 1940, Hitler ordered his top army brass to start preparing a massive surprise attack on Russia, which was codenamed 'Operation Barbarossa', after the 12th century King of Germany, Frederick Barbarossa, who had successfully captured much land for the country. It was to be launched on 2,900 km of frontage with three armies: Army Group North, Army Group Center and Army Group South.

Mobilization was the key to success and hence, during the preparatory stage itself, Germany stockpiled half a million tons of fuel, 91,000 tons of ammunition, 600,000 trucks and 750,000 horses to carry material. The operation was to be launched in May 1941, but Hitler had to postpone it by a month due to a commitment in North Africa. Timing was very critical because by August end, Russia would be hit by heavy rains, creating an ocean of slush, which, in turn, would make mobility very difficult. By October, Russia would become a freezing hell due to heavy snow. The Germans, therefore, had a very small window of time to go for an all-out attack if the operation was to launch in 1941. On 22 June 1941 just before 3 a.m., the USSR was shaken up with the largest bombardment in the history of warfare, with 20,000 artillery guns pounding the Red Army with thousands of tons of shells. With more than 3,000 aircraft, Luftwaffe (the German air force) gave the Soviets hell and supported mechanized attack on the ground. The initial victory was spectacular as Hitler's armies advanced up to 600 miles, 360,000 Soviet soldiers were killed and around a million injured, coupled with double the number captured.

However, as bad weather started building up, German armies started feeling the pressure. Though they had gained an advantage, they lost 550,000 men by September 1941 and

750,000 by December, including those who were missing in action. Partisans and the weather disrupted the supply line. Moreover, Germans soldiers had uniforms and equipment for mild winters and no ECC (Extreme Cold Climate) clothing was given to them. The frontage stretched across 1,800 miles (2,880 km) from the Black Sea to the Arctic. The initial blitzkrieg-like euphoria vanished within a few months and the Germans were battered by the Soviets as well as the weather within a few months of the attack. The principle of concentration of force, which had worked well before, was abandoned and the entire German force became too thin. Since all the three army groups were moving on different axes, though in tandem, their supply lines were obviously different, as their key objectives were Moscow, Leningrad and Ukraine respectively.

The German high command had underestimated not only the tenacity of the Soviet soldiers, but also their ability to mobilize more troops into the battle zone. As the Germans smashed a hundred Soviets, they brought in a hundred more. The Germans could not get anything intact when they captured the cities because of the scorched earth policy adopted by the Soviets, taking what they could and destroying the rest. The Soviets had perfected the art of removing industrial equipment and even whole factories so that Germans could not get them. They would reinstall these factories in the rear so that production for war-related material would not be hampered.

Without realizing the importance of mobilization and logistics, Hitler changed his objectives several times. The GS was not clear as to what the prime objective was—Moscow or Ukraine. Military commanders wanted to go for Moscow first so as to take advantage of the weather and momentum, but Hitler overruled this and asked to capture Leningrad, Ukraine and then Moscow. Though Ukraine was captured by September, the doors to Moscow were closed, because by then, their monsoon had set in, making the German movement extremely slow. The Soviets reinforced their army by replenishing their stocks in and around Moscow to give a tough fight to the Germans, who were by now exhausted and had limited fuel or ammunition to retaliate.

Hitler even came up with a funny idea to attack Moscow under these circumstances by making 'a final effort of willpower'. The mechanized army found it difficult to even move, as engines wouldn't start due to the severe cold and the artillery could not fire a shell. Food was hard to come by, and the Germans ate their dead frozen horses or even their own dead comrades.

The Soviet army had the capacity to take on the massive onslaught by the Germans. It had raised more than 820 divisions' equivalent of manpower and created replenishments very quickly. The Germans grossly underestimated the Soviet capability, especially their mobilization potential. Moreover, the Germans were not prepared for a long war; they thought that like blitzkrieg campaigns conducted earlier, this would also conclude quickly. Therefore, due to the prolonged war and deep penetration, the German army could not get the supplies required for victory. Tanks and other transport did not have the fuel even to reach their destination! The Germans had factored a good railway and road network in their plans, which failed miserably on ground, as German and Soviet railways had different sizes, and roads that looked good on the map during summers but became useless by the time monsoon arrived.

Operation Barbarossa was a failure. Though technically it was over by the beginning of December 1941, the fighting continued thereafter. By January 1942, Germany had lost 900,000 men in uniform.

Lessons Learnt from Barbarossa:

- Mobilization is the key to success for a large military or industrial campaign.
- Precision in planning can make even an extremely large operation successful.
- Since mobility is critical, planning should not be done from maps alone; other intelligence inputs must also be used.
- The principle of concentration of force must be kept in mind, and the resources should never get thinned out.
- You cannot win based on willpower alone.
- Operations must be executed as per the plans. No mid-course changes should be made.
- Delayed project execution due to external factors may incur a heavy price.
- The 'core tenet' must be identified while planning any military or commercial project. Wherever the core tenet is mobilization, full attention and priority must be given to it.
- Weather plays a very important part in any operation, civil or military.
- Never overstretch your supply lines.

Operation Overlord: Amphibious Invasion across the English Channel (6 June–25 August 1944)

Within the first year of the Second World War, Germany had defeated and captured France and almost the entire Europe. The Germans took Poland first, and then the Netherlands, Belgium, Luxembourg, France, Denmark, Yugoslavia, Greece, Norway and Western Poland. However, halted by the English

Channel, they were unable to invade England, which lay across this 560 km-long natural obstacle.

The US, Russia and England decided to liberate Europe by launching an attack across the English Channel. They landed first in France and then moved on to liberate the rest of Europe, with the final objective of defeating Germany. This was conceived and agreed upon in 1942, but was executed only in the middle of 1944.

This military invasion of Western Europe was codenamed 'Operation Overlord', and was a joint operation in which several nations participated. It was also a tri-service operation involving the army, navy and air force. The latter maintained air supremacy and gave support to ground troops, while the navy provided the ships and landing craft to move across the channel, carrying troops, tanks and all other equipment. The army was tasked to capture the beaches, make beachheads, break through German defenses and move into France, delivering a massive blow to the German forces.

It was a difficult, costly and risky campaign in terms of man and material, since the Germans were fully fortified in pill boxes, trenches and bunkers on the French side. The major task was to first have the entire fighting force at one place. It was also important to have the war equipment, arms, ammunition and other hardware in place, on the British soil. The Americans had built a very strong production base whereas the British did not have sufficient capacity to supply military hardware. Therefore, a joint hardware pool was created. The British took the responsibility for structuring and organizing the build-up phase, and the Americans produced and shipped the material. America also provided a huge fighting force for the entire war and this operation. General Dwight Eisenhower of the US army was the supreme commander of the Allied forces, while General Montgomery of the British Army was the commander of the land forces, who envisaged a 90-day battle to dislodge the Germans. British General F.E. Morgan was chief of staff to Eisenhower. Coordinating forces from different countries and involving the three services was a big challenge. General C.H. Lee of the US army was made in charge of logistics for the entire operation and he had a battery of logisticians under him. Spearheaded by General Morgan, the operation was the longest amphibious invasion in history, with 160,000 soldiers landing on D-Day across the channel.

This assault across the English Channel was codenamed 'Operation Neptune' and is popularly known as the Normandy Landings. The major strategic decision was to identify the best place to land. The Allied forces had two options. The first option was to take the shortest route across the channel and invade Calais over a distance of under 56 km. Calais was heavily defended by the Germans due to its proximity. The second option was to land at Normandy, which had a larger and broader landing area. However, it was at a longer distance and had a logistical problem. Since Normandy appeared difficult, the only port to land was Cherbourg, which was also heavily defended by the Germans. General Montgomery wanted to assault on a broader frontage alongside the Cherbourg port on the beaches of Normandy, and hence Normandy was the considered choice. The assault was planned on five beaches east of Cherbourg, situated across 80 km, and was to begin on 6 June 1944 at 6 a.m.

The Allied forces obviously did not want the Germans to know when and where the attack was coming from. In June 1944, a massive deception plan was made and executed during the build-up to the Normandy Landings. It was codenamed 'Bodyguard'. This was a general strategy to mislead Hitler and the German armed forces regarding the exact location and date of the invasion. Wrong messages were fed to the German high command to confuse them regarding the landings. In addition, deception was carried out by using German double agents and false wireless messages. Moreover, a sudden, massive troop movement could have given out the plan and alerted the Germans. Therefore the troops were moved into Britain gradually over a period of time. Under 'Operation Fortitude', two fake armies were also created, giving the impression that the attack could be launched at Calais or somewhere north in Norway. Dummy aircraft, tanks and guns made of wood and canvas were deployed. Due to this uncertainty, the Germans wanted to defend the entire coastline and their forces got thinned out. Even as the attack was building up at Normandy, the Germans thought it to be a feint or deceptive measure and kept their main task force far away.

A total of three airborne divisions and five infantry and armoured divisions were to take part in the initial assault. The British and Canadian divisions were to attack the eastern flank, the American forces the western side.

On D-Day, the assault began with the landing of over 160,000 troops at the Normandy beaches along an 80 km stretch, which was divided into five sectors: Utah, Omaha (US), Gold, Sword (UK) and Juno (Canadian). One lakh ninety thousand Allied naval and merchant navy personnel in over 5,000 ships and landing craft were involved in the massive assault across the channel.

The operation was conducted in two phases. First, an airborne assault landed 24,000 British, American and Canadian paratroops shortly after midnight on 5 June, while the second was the amphibious landing of the infantry and armoured divisions across five locations on the Normandy beaches. To deceive Hitler, two more decoy landings were done across the channel simultaneously, codenamed 'Glimmer' and 'Taxable'.

Since there was a shortage of harbours at Normandy, the British manufactured prefabricated portable harbours codenamed 'Mulberry'. On 9 June, just three days after the landings, two such harbours were taken in small sections across the English Channel and assembled at the beaches. They were used to land over 2.5 million men, 500,000 vehicles and 4 million tons of supplies, providing all the reinforcements in France for almost a year.

Since it was a mobile operation where Allied tanks and vehicles were to move across Europe, a huge amount of fuel was required by them. Carrying fuel in tanker ships across the channel was susceptible to bad weather as well as enemy attack. Therefore, the British armed forces, in association with oil companies, constructed undersea oil pipelines to pump fuel across the channel. These were first tested in the Bristol Channel and then deployed for actual operation. Pump stations on both sides were camouflaged as cottages or garages to avoid air attack.

Lessons Learnt:

- There must be a centralized command for strategic decisions while operating with forces (the army, navy and air force) from different countries. General Eisenhower was, therefore, appointed as the supreme commander of the Allied forces.

- All logistics should be centralized with sufficient decentralization.
- Detailed planning and rehearsals pay rich dividends.
- Weather can become a major factor when any operation is launched.
- It is better to have permanent methods of supply in case operations are going to be for a longer period. The British laid pipelines across the channel to supply fuel, rather than depending on ships or any other means of transportation.
- Deception is the key to success. Keeping such a large force under wraps is very difficult and therefore, all means of deception and deceit need to be applied simultaneously.

The Falklands War: A Naval and Military Operation
(2 April–14 June 1982)

The Falklands War was triggered when Argentina's military regime decided to occupy three British islands, i.e. the Falkland Islands, Sandwich and South Georgia located in South Atlantic Ocean. Britain had to conduct a war 13,000 km away from its own shores and it was primarily a naval operation supported by the army and air force. In the beginning, the British were not very optimistic about the outcome of this conflict because of the long operating distance from their homes. Hence, they used the island of Ascension as a forward base since it was located almost halfway through. Moreover, they had no military resources on Falkland Islands and had to bring everything with them from England. This naval air operation depended upon the smooth coordination of logistics across a very long distance.

As a military force, Argentina was much inferior to the British, but they had the advantage of being close to where the action was.

The British forces carried 9,000 personnel, 400,000 tons of fuel and more than 100,000 tons of material, and Americans provided them with aviation fuel on this forward base.

In this 10-week war, the British lost four ships (frigates and destroyers), and more than 30 helicopters and fighter aircraft.

Lessons Learnt:

- Fighting a war far off from the home base is very costly in terms of the loss of men and material.
- Mobilization of military hardware is not only expensive but requires precise coordination between the army, air force and navy.
- A forward base in such a situation, if established, can become a lifeline for any civil or military operation.

The Kargil War: High Altitude (May–July 1999)

This armed conflict between the two countries started because of infiltration by Pakistani militants into the Indian side of the Line of Control (LOC). Kargil is strategically important for India because the road connecting Srinagar to Leh passes through this sector. Ridges at Kargil overlook this road. It is the only connection between the mainland and Leh, which further leads to the Siachen area. Therefore, the entire supply line to the Indian troops in this area can get affected if this highway is blocked. The military outposts on the Kargil ridges overlooking the highway are 16,000–18,000 ft high. Anyone who occupies these positions would enjoy the advantage of a vantage point and also the protection of a fortress. Therefore, both the Pakistani and the Indian armies have their forward posts located in this area on their respective side of the LOC. During winter, both armies abandon some of the forward posts, only to reoccupy these during summer.

In 1999, Pakistanis planned to occupy some of the Indian posts during the winter season so as to dominate and block the highway, thus choking the supplies to Siachen. It was expected that due to this, Indians would have to withdraw from Siachen, which would help Pakistan to negotiate the 'Kashmir issue' in their favour.

During summers, the Indian army patrol used to be scaled up. In the second week of May 1999, one of the Indian patrolling parties was ambushed, which led to the discovery of Pakistani militants who were occupying Indian positions. Assuming that these were jihadis, the field commanders were of the view that they would be able to evict them within a few days. But once the initial effort to evict them was met by heavy resistance, they realized that Pakistanis had infiltrated on a much larger scale and with a definite purpose to block the all-important Srinagar-Leh highway. Pakistanis had done thorough planning and had reconnoitered the area using unmanned aerial vehicles.

India responded by mobilizing 200,000 troops in and around this area. In a matter of days, two divisions and the air force were deployed, totaling more than 30,000 troops. The number of infiltrators was estimated at about 5,000. For a decisive victory in mountain warfare, the attacking force needs to overwhelmingly outnumber the defender. Restrictions posed by the terrain eventually led to fierce battles in the high-altitude areas, which had very steep cliffs that were extremely difficult to negotiate. Most of the attacks came under heavy enemy fire from well-protected bunkers on higher ground. The Indian Air Force also supported the ground attacks, pressing into service 60 frontline aircraft. Very few airstrips were available, which limited the number of sorties further; it could not bring down the firepower because of the high altitude and weather conditions.

Tololing and Tiger Hill were to be neutralized first, because that would relieve the Srinagar-Leh roadway. Later, the Batalik sector was captured to open up the Siachen route. Both sides suffered heavy casualties in these battles. The war also witnessed hand-to-hand combat, which is rare in modern warfare. Frontal attacks had to be launched because the Indian forces were not allowed to encircle the enemy, as this would have resulted in their crossing over the LOC to enter Pakistani soil, which could have resulted in a full-blown war between the two.

The only option to capture Tololing was to launch a frontal attack with full artillery support. To pulverize the enemy, 120 artillery guns pounded this area of the ridge with shells equivalent to 50,000 of TNT that could have devastated a large city. The battalions involved in the attack conducted mock drills on ridges similar to Tololing to get an idea of the degree of difficulty in undertaking such an operation. The attacks were mostly by night, as daytime would have been suicidal for troops who were vulnerable to enemy fire. For a fit and fully acclimatized soldier, it would take more than 10 hours to climb those heights. Indian forces lost more than 500 men and had more than 1,300 wounded, costing the country an estimated ₹10,000 crore or US $2,000 million.

Several historians opine that Kargil may have been a tactical success, but was a strategic failure.

Lessons Learnt:

- Unmanned posts due to inclement weather must be monitored using high-tech equipment. Pakistan used unmanned aerial vehicles to reconnoiter the area before it started the process of infiltration. In the business scenario, it is good to keep an ear on the ground to identify threats to the business. It is also important to keep a track of market changes. In today's scenario, this needs to be done almost in real time.

- High-altitude mountain warfare requires massive outnumbering of the enemy in terms of manpower to achieve any objective.
- You need to have multiple roads and approaches as supply lines to critical areas. Depending on one—as in the case of the Srinagar-Leh road—can lead the adversary to hold you to ransom.
- The air force and airlifting are not very effective in high-altitude scenarios.
- Mobilization of men and material in high-altitude areas is extremely difficult and costly.
- In mountains, the advance stocking of ammunition and food is an inescapable requirement.

The Burma Campaign: Jungle Warfare (January 1942–July 1945)

Jungle warfare is a term that emerged during the Second World War. The Vietnam War, the Burma campaign and even the Korean War are some major wars that had been fought in jungles. The Indian Peace Keeping Force also fought the Liberation Tigers of Tamil Eelam in the dense jungles of Sri Lanka.

Jungle terrain requires not only different types of tactics, but also different types of logistical support. A soldier not only fights the human enemy, but also has to fight a second enemy—the jungle itself. Since this difficult environment is applicable to friend and foe both, the side that can better deal with the jungle would have a distinct advantage over the other.

Jungles comprise thick undergrowth and a highly dense cover of trees. From the mobilization point of view, this makes movement difficult. Very few roads are available for carrying equipment, food and clothing. Special efforts are required to manage tropical and water-borne diseases. Suffocating heat, insufficient sunlight, humidity and heavy rains also make the life of a soldier very hard.

The Burma campaign was a long-drawn war between the Axis powers, i.e. the Japanese supported by the Indian National Army and Thailand, and the Allies, i.e. the British supported by the Chinese, Canadians and the US. The British forces were primarily from the Indian Army.

The Japanese had invaded Burma with the objective of blocking the supply line to China. Without British and American support via the Burma road, China would not have been able to fight the Japanese forces. The Japanese had made considerable advances and were able to expel the Allies from Burma. The Allies, on the other hand, made considerable effort (they wanted to keep China in the war to keep the Japanese engaged), but were unable to recapture most of their lost ground between 1942 and 1943. In 1944, the Japanese invaded India, but were halted at Kohima and Imphal. At this point, the tide turned and the Allies struck back to recapture Burma by the middle of 1944. This war continued for more than three years, because the British had to accord higher priority to the war with Germany in the west.

The supply line had to depend on military engineers to build roads and bridges, as Burma lacked road infrastructure.

The Japanese very cleverly used a bicycle infantry, which could move without making any sound and operate on narrow semi-constructed roads or pathways. These cycles were very light, and could be folded and airdropped along with the paratroopers. Air transport was another means to evacuate the wounded and also provide critical equipment. Due to heavy rains, the battles could be fought only for about six months in a year. Lord Mountbatten took charge of the Allied forces in 1943 and due to his influence, could manage to get transport aircraft to augment the air supply for the forward troops.

To circumvent the problem of mobilization in large numbers, the British, under the leadership of Brigadier Orde Wingate, created a special task force that could operate deep behind the enemy lines. They were a self-contained, physically tough and well-trained force of 3,000 men. Brigadier Wingate trained them in the jungles of Central India during heavy rains so as to familiarize them with the jungle terrain. He was also the one who came up with the theory of long-range penetration, with a view to disrupt communications and hit at the enemy's vital points. This 'special force' was called Chindits, named after mythical beasts, statues of which guard Buddhist temples.

In February 1943, the first expedition of Chindits was called 'Operation Long Cloth', whereby these 3,000 men marched across 1,000 miles in the thick jungles of Burma, relying only on scant air droppings that could be managed infrequently at predetermined locations. These forces typically operated in small formations called 'columns.' Each man carried more than 30 kg of equipment, weapons, ammunition and rations. Many times while moving through these thick jungles, they cleared the ground foliage with khukris and machetes to make a pathway.

'Operation Thursday' was launched in March 1944 with 20,000 men. This second Chindit operation used aircraft to transport men and equipment. At preselected open fields in Burma, advance troops landed in gliders that made no sound and prepared the airfields for large-scale landings by transport aircraft. More than 10,000 men were transported by air.

Though the Chindits lost more than 1,300 men and many were wounded, they contributed immensely to the Allied victory against Japan.

Lessons Learnt:

- In jungle warfare, supply by air is very effective and hence, airports and aircraft must be adequately available.
- To gather a larger force, advance parties must be landed in open fields first and then these fields must be prepared as airfields.
- Innovative ways of transportation can be effectively used in the jungle terrain. Cycles and special commando task forces that can walk for hundreds of miles as a self-contained force are examples. Training in a simulated environment (as done by Wingate in Central India) can help during the actual operation.

The North African Campaign: Libyan and Egyptian Deserts
(10 June 1940–13 May 1943)

Mobilization, logistics and supply line management are critical in modern warfare and the North African Campaign is a glaring example of this theory. Since the late 19th century, many Western countries had their interests in North Africa. Italian forces were present in Libya and the British were located in Egypt, the neighbouring country.

On 10 June 1940, Italy entered the Second World War by declaring war on Britain and France. Almost immediately, skirmishes started between the Italians and the British in this region. In September 1940, the Italians realized that Britain was being battered in the Battle of Britain on their home turf, and this was the best time to nail them in this region. They, therefore, attacked and captured some areas that were under the British. However, Operation Compass, a massive counter-offensive, was launched by the British, which destroyed a major portion of the Italian 10th Army. This is the time when Hitler sent Field Marshal Erwin Rommel with his Africa corps to reinforce the Italian Army. A series of battles between the Italians and Germans (Axis), and the British along with Americans, Australians and Canadians (Allies) took place to exercise control over Libya and Egypt. General Bernard Montgomery of the British Army was the commander of the Allied forces in this region.

The battles were mostly for the port towns, so that the supply line could be managed. Alexandria was a port on one end of Egypt and Tripoli was one on the other end. In between these two, there was a string of ports—Benghazi, Tobruk and El Alamein.

Two brilliant generals, Montgomery and Rommel, were pitched against each other. The former had the distinct advantage of having more resources like tanks, aircraft and guns. The Germans, on the other hand, had supply shortages, especially fuel, which was so important in tank warfare. They could have mobilized more tanks and guns, but without the supply of fuel, there would have been no specific advantage.

Rommel's Africa corps had three armoured/mechanized divisions, three infantry divisions and four Italian divisions.

This required a supply of more than 70,000 to 80,000 tons of supply per month, including food, ammunition and fuel. All this was to be provided through the sea route and unloaded at major ports. Since Tripoli was in depth, it could work at its full capacity of handling around 30,000 tons per month. Benghazi was closer to the front where the actual battles were being fought. It was under constant bombing and could only handle 10,000–15,000 tons a month. Thus, Rommel was always short of supplies. In addition, the supplies had to be moved entirely through one road, right from Tripoli to the frontline, causing unacceptable delays, as it was exposed to enemy air attacks and ground raids. Limited rail lines were available to Rommel, which also led to a shortage of rolling stock. The warring sides had to flip flop between Tripoli and Alexandria—a distance of 1,900 km. Almost half the fuel was consumed by the trucks that supplied fuel and water.

In comparison, the British had a larger fleet of trucks for supplies and also better rail road. Much of the water was supplied through pipelines, which reduced the load on truck-based water tankers. They also had the ability to lay new rail lines, which the Germans failed to do.

Though Rommel was called the 'Desert Fox' for his brilliant tank warfare in this campaign, due to poor logistics, the Germans eventually lost. The North African Campaign is the best illustration of the US Marine Corps doctrine: 'Logistics establishes limits on what is operationally possible.'

Lessons Learnt:

- Even if you have enough machinery, you need to have energy to run it. Tanks, trucks and aircraft are useless pieces of hardware in war, unless they get a constant supply of fuel.

- Mobilization is an 'end to end' game plan like a jigsaw puzzle; every piece must fall in place for it to succeed. The carrying capacity of ships as well as the offloading arrangements at ports are both important.
- The ability to locally extend roads and railways is an added advantage.
- For prolonged operations, it is better to build infrastructure like pipelines to carry fuel and water. This can help reduce substantial transportation load.

Key Lessons in Mobilization

- Mobilization is the key to success for any military operation. It is also an essential component for business operations, which depend on large-scale manpower and material.
- While planning any operation, mobilization must be a part of the executive plan.
- Mobilization must follow the principle of concentration of force. Never let resources get thinned out.
- Contingency plans must be integrated in the overall mobilization plan.
- Control should be centralized at the highest level with sufficient decentralization built into it.
- Coordination with all stakeholders is the key to a successful mobilization plan and its smooth execution.

Logistics and Mobilization for Disaster Management

In comparison to any other operation conducted by civilians, disaster management probably comes closest to military operations. Several similarities can be identified and some of the lessons learnt from military operations can be cleverly adapted.

Disasters across the world take many forms and can strike any region of a country. Earthquakes, floods, hurricanes, tsunamis, tornados, volcanic eruptions, wildfires and ice storms are examples and each throws up its own unique challenges.

One Size Does Not Fit All

All disasters are destructive and mostly unpredictable in nature, creating a situation that needs immediate action. They affect the local population, which requires immediate and sustainable help. Challenges posed by disasters are similar to the ones posed during military operations. The mobilization of relief teams and material is one of the most critical aspects. Terrain and weather have to be considered while planning a relief operation as hills, jungles and deserts pose different challenges. Relief material is required to be procured according to different climatic conditions as well. Snow, heat and rains dictate how much relief equipment and men can be mustered and how fast they can be moved.

Again, like a military operation where full and authentic information about the enemy is not available, appropriate information regarding prevailing local conditions may not be available to relief agencies, due to the destruction of communication networks, roads and other means of transportation.

Therefore, like military operations, 'one size fits all' does not hold good even in disaster management. Every situation is different and every disaster has its own challenges, which may require a different response.

Coordination and Focus Are the Keys to Success

When different countries join a bloc to fight a common enemy, military operations face the problem of coordination. In addition, each country may have its own agenda and political philosophy, making things difficult at the operational level. A similar situation may be faced in a disaster. For example, an NGO like the Red Cross may look at a disaster from a humane angle, while a neighbouring nation may pour in aid to build bonds and do it entirely for political leverage. One NGO may address the issue of community stability while the other may have a religious overtone. Certain organizations use this opportunity to promote thier own brand and get into 'one-upmanship'. Some organizations involved in disaster management may look at this as a 'photo opportunity,' seeking media attention.

Coordination between different relief agencies is very important and is usually lacking in such relief operations. This is well streamlined in the armed forces and must be taken as a major learning from the military. Disaster management must have a central command and control structure like the military. In today's scenario, there is more available than can be utilized, in terms of funding, relief material and number of men and women available from different organizations to enthusiastically get involved in relief operations. Cooperation and coordination, therefore, are important.

Advance Planning and Provisioning

Logistics and the mobilization of resources is fundamental to disaster management. The International Red Cross has identified this and has created stockpiles required for immediate relief. This stockpile can cater to 300,000 people for one month, and located in different regions of the world as units that can immediately respond to a disaster situation. They also have a policy regarding donations, transport planning and even prioritizing the inventory.

Though a lot is being done to handle and manage disasters, a comprehensive set of principles acceptable across the board have yet not been fully devised. While formulating these guidelines, the military principles of logistics and mobilization could be intelligently adapted.

The Dubai Palm Islands: An Example of Successful Mobilization in a Business Venture

The brainchild of the current ruler of Dubai, Sheikh Mohammed bin Rashid, the Palm Islands are an engineering marvel that required a massive mobilization of manpower and material. Sheikh Mohammad was aware of the dwindling oil reserves in his country and had to look for an alternate source of earning for his people. Since Dubai is a tourist destination, he wanted to further capitalize on this by augmenting the length of the beaches of Dubai, which only had a 72 km shoreline. He thus came up with the idea of building an artificial island connected to the mainland.

Initially, a circular island was proposed by the engineers. Since this would not have maximized the beach length, Sheikh Mohammed himself came up with the design of a palm tree. This was a tribute to the date palm tree, abundant in the region, and also called the 'bride of orchard' in the Gulf. In addition, it was a brilliant idea, a geometrical shape to maximize the peripheral length of the beach frontage. The first of such islands, Palm Jumeirah, was to have 17 fronds extending from a tree trunk, which was to be surrounded by an 11.5 km-long breakwater crescent to protect the artificial shoreline. This alone was to add 78 km to the existing shoreline.

More than a hundred studies in different engineering disciplines were carried out before the project started, as the region was in a seismic zone with 6–7 richter scale predictability. Construction started in June 2001 and the massive effort to construct the first residential tenement, which could have ordinarily taken 15 years, was ready within a record five years in 2006.

It required 9.5 million m^3 of sand and 7 million tons of rocks. Some of the rock pieces weighed more than 6 tons. Sheikh Mohammed desired that only natural material like sand and stone be used, so that the island would not have a negative impact on the environment. This made the task more difficult, because the sand available in the deserts of Dubai was too fine for the job as it would not hold together in water and get swept away by the sea. Therefore, the engineers had to get sand out of the oceanbed using dredging equipment. A 40,000-plus workforce was employed, which often worked in temperatures as high as 48°C in double shifts to complete this task. This project was planned and executed by 1,200 engineers. The breakwater was like a 200 m-broad, 3 m-high necklace around the island, which was built to protect the islands from the lashing waves of water and also storms. The work could only progress when the sea was calm and this was a constraint against the deadline.

More than 120,000 people were to live here. As a tourist destination, 28 luxury hotels were built, 12,000 palm trees were planted and a monorail commissioned for transportation. It was to have 220 malls, 8,000 villas and 450 luxury apartments.

The execution was carried out like a military operation. The project managers also faced problems similar to the ones faced in real time during war. For instance, after the breakwater ring was in place, they realized that there was no way for fresh seawater to enter the shores of the island. This would have made the water stagnant and stale, so they had to cut open two channels in the ring to let in the freshwater to tide over this problem.

The Attitude and Habit of Building a Reserve

Men in uniform are taught to cultivate the habit of building a reserve. Serving in different geographical locations teaches different life skills. For instance, while travelling in high-altitude areas, they encounter sudden heavy rainfall, flash floods, landslides and snow storms. The weather is unpredictable and a bright sunny afternoon can well turn into a nightmare in just a few hours. One may also get stuck in a location for days due to a natural calamity. Whenever you move out, the dictum therefore is as follows: 'One meal in the stomach, one meal and some dry rations in the backpack.' It is good to cultivate the habit of being prepared all the time.

Manpower Planning

While planning for manpower in any business, an optimum reserve is one of the most important and difficult tasks. Most industrialized economies have witnessed a shift towards the service sector. Today, 70 per cent of the US economy is based on the service industry, which is highly manpower dependent. This trend is being witnessed all over the world. For instance, in the Indian scenario, the IT industry spends almost half of its revenue on manpower as staffing cost.

Demand by clients in the IT sector is quite volatile and therefore, a concept of inbuilt reserve is followed by most companies. In India, a progressive IT company therefore, keeps almost 10–20 per cent manpower on the 'bench', to be readily available and deployed as and when required for a new project. This should also be able to absorb the unpredictable attrition. Since technical manpower is relatively cheaper in Asian countries, a comfortable reserve can be built in. In the Western context, this reserve may shrink between 5 to 10 per cent.

Airlines across the world have to keep their fleet flying for a maximum time. Any 'downtime' is very expensive and will eat into their profits. Besides keeping the aircraft 'flying fit,' a big challenge is the availability of an adequate number of pilots. The cockpit crew again accounts for a major part of the operating expense in airline businesses. Besides having regular pilots, an airline also has to keep a reserve pool. While the regular pilots are optimally utilized (as their schedules are very much planned in advance), the reserve pool needs to be managed with due diligence to avoid overstaffing, as this would result in the underutilization of the reserve pool. In the US, certain airlines keep a reserve pool of 20 per cent upwards.

Therefore, for a business, the top management must keep an ample reserve to meet the unforeseen demands, depending on the industry sector it is operating in. This allows the organization to respond to unpredictable market dynamics and retain its competitive edge by meeting client deadlines. This way, no new business opportunity is ever lost. Many facility-management companies maintain a 'commando group' that can be rapidly deployed for new projects. Once the initial phase is over, fresh manpower is recruited and deployed for the project, thus relieving the commando group to be deployed for similar assignments elsewhere.

Financial Planning: Cash Reserve

Even at a personal level, one is advised to keep a reserve to last for four to six months. This money is for those hard days when one's other sources of income have dried up. The cardinal principle is to never touch this reserve until and unless it is an emergency, just like military GS reserve.

In business finance, the rule of thumb is to keep an adequate cash flow reserve. This translates into figures depending on the market scenario and the industry in which the company operates. After the 2008 global financial crisis, most companies became very cautious and held cash on their balance sheets, which was more than that of the previous years. The crisis taught them that to have flexibility and to survive a crisis, there is no better way than a cash reserve pile sitting on the budget sheets.

The 2008 crisis was triggered by several factors, one of which was that companies got too aggressive and reckless while the going was good. Unfortunately, at both the personal and professional levels, people become reckless and throw caution out of the window, only to regret it later.

10

Teeth-to-Tail Ratio: Maximum Bang for the Buck

> '*A piece of spaghetti or a military unit can be led only from the front end.*'
> —George S. Patton

The Basic Concept

Most wars are waged to capture enemy land comprising cities, industries and agricultural resources. Warfare is a complex affair involving several elements working together. In a battlefield, there are some troops who are directly involved in combat. They are usually right in the front and are responsible for capturing enemy territory. The combatants are from the infantry and the armoured corps, which is a tank-based force. Today, in almost every modern army, a large portion of infantry is provided transportation for quick mobility in the battlefield. The troops are usually carried in APCs, which are as agile as tanks and have armour to protect them from enemy firing.

There are a large number of resources in terms of men and material, which are required to support these combat personnel on a continuous basis. In army parlance, they are the support arms and services who are also in the combat zone but are there to provide support and are not usually tasked to attack and capture enemy personnel and territory.

Artillery, as a supporting arm, provides the firepower and works in conjunction with the fighting forces. Similarly, combat engineers provide bridges, roads, waterworks and signals. They are responsible for providing end-to-end battlefield communication. There are also support services like supply corps for fuel and food. Electronics and mechanical engineers cater to repairs of all military hardware. The ordnance corps provides and replenishes the entire military hardware including clothing. And the medical corps provides medical cover right from the frontline to the large hospitals located in depth.

One would appreciate that all these elements have their own relevance and therefore, no military operation is possible if even one of the elements is missing or underperforms. At a macro level, these elements can be divided into two parts: one that is actually involved in combat is termed as the 'teeth' and the other that is in a supporting role is termed as the 'tail'. The tail is complex and is responsible for the entire logistical support for the fighting elements, i.e. infantry and armoured corps. The ability to deliver a punch or actually bite into the enemy flesh lies with the teeth. But the teeth cannot bite unless there is support of the entire jaw, i.e. the tail.

If one observes an athlete throwing a javelin, one can easily conclude that it is not the arm of the athlete alone that is responsible for the throw but instead, every part of the body—the torso, legs and feet. If the legs fail to build up the fight, the throw will never be good enough. Similarly, the torso has its own role to play. Something similar happens in golf, wherein a player uses his entire body, and not only his arms or wrists, to hit the ball. If one observes animals, they use their tails in several different ways and for many good reasons. Some species of kangaroos use their tails for balance, whereas monkeys and opossums have prehensile tails that they use for grasping branches as they swing along. Some types of lizards can detach and throw away their tails to distract their enemy, providing them an opportunity to escape. Back home, dogs show their emotions by wagging their tails.

In the battleground, the 'teeth to tail' ratio could well be taken as a measure of how much bang for the buck you can get from your armed forces. Since it is a ratio between what comprises the teeth and how big the tail is, the effort would always be to optimize this figure. The only way is to shorten the tail as much as possible. Although the concept looks simple and is universal, its interpretation and usefulness would differ from country to country. The armed forces are an integral part of a sovereign state. Nation states in different political situations have different geographical interests and very divergent political objectives and military strategies. Therefore, a 'one size fits all' kind of an analysis may not be possible. Yet, some very basic axioms can be concluded from which armed forces and their controlling ministries can learn to deliver more output with lesser inputs—in short, more for less.

For instance, if an army has to fight far away from home, on a different land, then its logistical support mechanism will be very different and much more elaborate from what would be required to fight within its own borders. This was first experienced by the US during the Second World War, when they had to ship their men and material thousands of miles away into Europe. In this case, the tail literally became very long, fragmented and even vulnerable. Many lessons were learnt by the Americans and some of the learnings were applied during the Vietnam War in the 60s and the Gulf War in the 80s. The Germans paid a heavy price for neglecting their tail during the Russian Campaign and the North African Campaign during the Second World War. They not only lost vital territory, but also had very large casualties in these wars.

What Is the Teeth and What Is the Tail

For any military organization, the most difficult part of the exercise is to define the difference between elements that constitute the teeth and the ones that make the tail. Unfortunately, there is no standard international benchmark and the ratio can therefore be interpreted differently by different armies.

The flipside of this is that many armies and their political bosses started looking at the teeth and tail purely from the point of view of manpower. It then becomes a tool for downsizing the armed forces. This trend started after the Second World War when a large workforce became suddenly irrelevant and surplus. Governments wanted them quickly delisted and absorbed into civilian jobs to cut their defense budget spending. That is the time experts started thinking of retaining more teeth and doing away with a large portion of the tail, purely from the headcount point of view.

Let us view the idea from two different perspectives: one at a micro level and the other from the macro viewpoint. Let us also look at it from the manpower perspective alone to begin with.

Micro Level

The smallest independent organization in the army is a unit, which is a battalion or a regiment. A typical infantry battalion's capability is its 'bayonet strength,' which is the number of soldiers that will actually take part in an assault. In the US army, an infantry battalion has a total strength of 860 men. It has three rifle companies of 193 men each, which is the actual fighting force. This means that out of 860, only 579 are the teeth. The teeth-to-tail ratio works out to 2.1:1.

In a typical tank regiment, there are 45 tanks, six APCs that are combat vehicles and three armour recovery vehicles. There are 750 men in a regiment. The fighting force, distributed over these 45 tanks and six BMPs (short for Boyevaya Mashina Pekhoty, a Soviet amphibious tracked infantry fighting vehicle), comprises around 500 men. Therefore, 250 people are involved in the administrative role. In such a scenario, the teeth-to-tail ratio is, at best, 2:1.

Macro Level

For any large-scale rationalization, a macro-level picture may be more suited for analysis. As explained in the beginning of the chapter, the infantry and armoured forces are the teeth and the rest of the forces, though deployed very much simultaneously and collocated with them, form the tail. The artillery, which provides the entire long-range firepower, can be considered as either teeth or tail, and that can make a substantial difference in interpretation. Besides this, there are a number of civilian employees deployed at peace locations including the central headquarters like the Pentagon or the service headquarters.

In 2010, in a report by McKinsey, Scott Gebicke and Samuel Magid benchmarked the defence performances of different countries. They mapped data from 33 countries to show that in many armed forces, there is room to optimize the teeth-to-tail ratio. They divided the army personnel into three categories: the combatants comprising the infantry, armoured and combat aviation; the combat support including the artillery, engineers, signals and others; and other active duties (non-combatant) including the HR, IT, procurement and accounting. There was a huge variation from the best to the worst. On an average, the distribution was 26:11:63, which meant that for a teeth of 26, one had a tail of 74 (1:3).

Israel was one of the top fighting forces with 38:6:56 (38:62) or (1:1.6), China at 31:3:66 (31:69) or (1:2.2), Russia at 21:7:72 (21:79) or (1:3.76) and the US as 16:7:77 (16:84) or (1:5.25). So much variation itself shows that there is room for improvement. Probably the Chinese and Israeli armies are more frugal and require their frontline soldiers to expect much lesser comfort and remain self-contained than the Americans. This could be related to the culture of a country. As per the report, France stood at 16:8:76 (1:5.25), and is aiming at a dramatic reduction of administrative personnel by outsourcing some functions and investing in technology. Some northern European nations also want their teeth-to-tail ratio to improve by centralizing or pooling manpower.

Keeping manpower at the centre of the teeth-to-tail ratio would be foolhardy. Though armies spend a substantial amount on manpower including pensions, cutting on manpower may not give the optimum results. Modern armed forces fail to effect considerable reductions in manpower by substituting fighting personnel with innovative tenchnologies. Some armies have rampantly cut down the support manpower, creating ridiculous situations often resulting in more and more difficulties for a fighting soldier. This is true for those armies that are continuously deployed on borders or are involved in operations in foreign lands. They are under tremendous stress and making them more uncomfortable would negatively impact the efficiency of the entire system.

It also differs based upon the type of terrain and tactics. For instance, in the plains, army formations move very quickly, resulting in a longer tail of logistics, which need to catch up equally fast. Similarly, the tail is at times longer and always much harder to maintain in mountainous terrain. National security planners are constantly creating new ways to make 'affordable defense'. There is therefore a need to analyse the efficiency, based on how much you spend on what.

Efficiency and Effectiveness: The Larger Picture

Budget becomes the bottom line for defense as well as civil benchmarking. If it is bang for the buck, then buck it is. All armies have a large number of non-combatant civilians who are paid from the defense budget. It is important to consider their utilization for the overall effectiveness of the armed forces and they must be accounted for as part and parcel of the organization, as they consume resources and money. The operational effectiveness of the defense has to be ensured at all levels.

Let us consider the simplest efficiency or productivity of a machine model that one is so familiar with. It takes into account the input that goes into the machine and the total output that is generated. It is a ratio of output to the input that determines the efficiency. If the output is 80 and the input is 100, the efficiency is 0.8 or 80 per cent. This efficiency model assumes that the inefficiency stems out of some 'wasted' element due to the inefficiency of the system like friction, heat wastage, etc.

In case of a workforce like the armed forces, it would be better to take into account what is spent on the teeth and what is spent on the tail and look at that as an index of efficiency. An index of efficiency indicates the combat competitive edge of the armed forces of a nation over others, also known as the combat competitive index (CCI), which takes into account all expenses and lets you know how much bang for the buck you actually get. Therefore,

$$CCI = \text{Budget for the teeth} \div \text{Budget for the tail}$$

Budget for teeth: The core functions related to combat, manpower and new weapon systems. This includes force multipliers like battlefield information systems and any other expenses that directly enhance combat power.

Budget for tail: All other non-operational expenses that are non-combative in nature.

Therefore, if you spend more on the teeth than the tail (which includes manpower, equipment and maintenance) then the system moves towards being more efficient.

The expense heads have to be estimated in detail to decide what actually constitute the teeth expense. Once this is done, the rest of the budget is spent on the tail. A higher index is directly proportionate to better resource utilization, resulting in better combat power management, which gives a fighting force a competitive edge over others. This model takes care of everything, and not only manpower as misinterpreted many times to justify manpower cut.

Historical Perspective of Logistics and Support in Warfare

The logistics technique employed by Alexander the Great proves the old saying, 'Amateurs talk about strategy, but professionals discuss logistics.' Almost 2,500 years ago, the armies under the Macedonian empire were known for their lightning speed and surprise tactics. Alexander set many new benchmarks in warfare, one of them being efficient logistics management. He spent sufficient time and invested his thinking into managing his tail. He would supply forward bases with supplies by ships, which were then dismembered and carried overland to another river, to supply the next forward bases. During his numerous victories, Alexander accumulated a lot of spoils, which he realized could not be carried along if they were to maintain speed, which was almost 35 miles a day. He therefore, carried only whatever was necessary. He set fire to the wagons carrying his own luggage and then ordered all others to be burnt and left behind.

Alexander put in place certain basic principles of logistics. Simplicity was paramount in his planning. He always planned and used inputs from zoologists and botanists to assess the availability of fruits, grain and animals that could be obtained from the areas where he planned to attack. He established the concept of a single point of contact and gave this responsibility to a senior general. In specific situations, he also broke his army into smaller units so that they could become self-sustainable. This was required as they were asked to follow different routes and cities to reach the same destination.

Even today, many business and military institutions study his methods. During Operation Enduring Freedom to help Afghanistan get rid of the Taliban regime, the US forces also followed the dictum as practised by Alexander: 'Don't carry what you don't need.' They used DHL and FedEx services to move military hardware, achieving much larger teeth than the tail.

The Contemporary Scenario

In modern military operations, logistics and maintenance are colossal tasks. Speed, volume, uncertainty and risk are all at their peak. For the people involved in the task of logistics, the risk of getting injured or killed may be less, but the quantum and criticality of work is huge.

The Second World War

During the Second World War, military commanders experienced modern weapon systems and the enormity of forces. With tank warfare coming in, the German generals produced the idea of lightning warfare (blitzkrieg) where the tank force mauled the enemy and penetrated deep into the enemy territory. The fighting force was to be supported by the administrative echelons in terms of food and fuel, maintaining the same speed. At the same time, it was preplanned that the strike force would utilize all that was available in the occupied territory. Food, fuel dumps, shelters and communication systems were to be captured intact and fully utilized. In the battle for France, the Germans could therefore, manage well with limited administrative support of their own. In 1941, when they attacked the USSR, Stalin ordered his retreating forces to destroy everything that could be of any use to the Germans, as part of the scorched earth policy. Hence, the Germans didn't get any food or fuel. Millions suffered and hundreds of thousands of German soldiers starved to death. This was probably the first time that modern military commanders realized the importance of the tail.

The Vietnam War

In 1965, America got into the Vietnam War to support South Vietnam, which was fighting North Vietnam's communist Viet Minh party, which had the direct support of the Soviets. As Vietnam did not have the facilities to support the modern American army, the Americans spent close to $4 billion to construct roads, deep water ports, 200 large and small airfields and millions of square feet of refrigerated facilities, bridges and even oil pipelines and storage tanks. Within less than a year, there were 180,000 US soldiers in Vietnam and within four years at the peak of the conflict, the US committed 550,000 men for this conflict. Though the war conditions were horrible, the Americans ensured not only regular supplies of food and ammunition as required in battlefield conditions, but went miles ahead by providing the troops with lavish treatment. The opulent service included hot meals and decent living accommodation. The evacuation of the wounded to well-equipped hospitals was done in helicopters. At the peak of the battle, 197,000 injured were moved by air ambulances. The ratio of surviving to dead was 6:1 as compared to 2.6:1 of the Second World War.

The entire logistical support was established under a united command employing thousands of soldiers and Vietnamese civilians. For every combat soldier, there were five support personnel.

In contrast, the Ho Chi Minh army was resilient and could manage to live off the land. They had modest needs wherein the non-food requirement of a soldier was only 43 gm per day. At the peak of the war, the total requirement of the entire force was only 120 tons a day whereas a single American army division alone required five times of this amount!

The Americans were neither sure about the depth of the war nor about its length. Since everything was to be imported, the tail became very long and expensive. The American soldiers couldn't live on frugal support and their country gave them all that could be given in a war. This was a costly war for America on two counts. One, the Americans paid a heavy price as they lost countless men, the total casualties on their side being 15,000-plus killed and 100,000 wounded. Two, it cost them billions of dollars. As far as the teeth-to-tail ratio is concerned, the Americans spent much more lavishly on the tail as compared to other countries. For instance, they could have been more prudent about granting $4 billion to build infrastructure alone. Logistics does impact operational efficiency and the morale of the troops, but being lavish is unnecessary.

This has a sharp similarity with workforce management in the civilian context. The developed world hires talent from developing countries because they get cheap labour, almost at a fraction of that in their own country. People in developing countries are less demanding and are willing to work even in hard conditions. One would observe that many IT and ITES companies spend a lot on their talent pool. They try to retain them by giving plenty of 'freebies' such as free food, pick-up and drop facilities and recreational infrastructures like tennis and squash courts, and swimming pools. This is not the case in the manufacturing sector.

In the case of IT as well as manufacturing sectors, manpower is the basic ingredient, but IT makes these 'visible investments' more than manufacturing companies. The reasons for this difference could be several. First, when the IT boom hit the industry, there was a huge gap between demand and supply of qualified, productive manpower and companies had to resort to these 'luring tactics' to get people on board and then retain them. Second, initially the profit margins in IT companies were quite good and they could afford to spend such money on the workforce. In addition, as compared to the cost of workforce abroad, even after paying more than the manufacturing sector and giving additional perquisites, they still made good profits. Another reason could be that the investment in infrastructure like plant and real estate was colossal for manufacturing companies as compared to IT companies. Hence, they had to be frugal in their operational costs to strike a balance. One should also not discount the basic remuneration barrier between the white collar and the blue collar workforce that is required for these two industry sectors.

Operation Desert Storm: Gulf War

Once again, America had to fight the Gulf War far away from its shores. Here, the Americans used high technology and provided all the logistical support that was required for an operation of this mammoth size. The war was also conducted at a ferocious speed.

In Operation Beans, Bandages and Bullets, the US GS kept the lessons learnt in Vietnam in mind. While in Vietnam, the logistical build-up was a parallel activity to the operations (infrastructure was being built while the actual fighting was going on). In Operation Desert Storm, the build-up was done before the main battle commenced.

They applied Alexander's principle of centralized control and single point contact by making General Pagonis the head of the 22nd Support Command. Everything was routed through him with sufficient decentralization spread across the war theater. A 45-day intense war amounted close to $60 billion dollar for the US exchequer. Around 300 lives were lost and 460 injured. Of course, a very large portion of this expense was paid by the coalition countries and Saudi Arabia.

This war, in a way, was a logistic marvel where Pagonis and his staff handled 170,000 vehicles, including more than 10,000 tanks and APCs. They also had more than 12,500 aircraft of all types. In support of the ground troop on tanks and APCs, this 100-hour intense war employed more than 125,000 sorties of aircraft. Though the build-up took six months, the battle was wound up in 100 hours.

General Pagonis wanted to be flexible while planning all the phases of war. The Saudi ports were fed by ships coming from 65 ports worldwide. Time was a very important parameter and they could not afford bottlenecks at the unloading ports. Hence, they offloaded ships in 24 to 48 hours and if there was a backlog, they would ask ships at sea to slow down.

Although heat-and-eat meals were available in abundance, Pagonis wanted to boost the morale of the troops and contacted a wealthy Saudi businessman to supply hot meals, including hot dogs, pizzas and burgers, terming them 'A-Rations', to troops even at the frontline. More than 50 million meals were served by the administrative staff. They pumped in 1.3 billion gallons of fuel for the entire operation. In the words of Commander-General Norman Schwarzkopf, 'Logistic effort to mobilize was Herculean, especially a few weeks before the hostilities started.'

Many American lives were saved due to the advance build-up with robust logistics and high-technology weapon systems and by avoiding a long protracted war. This level of planning and execution could be very useful for planning any large-scale civil or military operation. While planning supplies, considering flexibility and the centralization of logistics are key issues. This will ensure the avoidance of duplicity and wastage of effort and material, while catering to everyone's needs. In his study called 'The Other End of the Spear,' John McGrath of the Combat Studies Institute, Kansas, says that the proportion of non-combatant elements has progressively increased from 1917 (under 50 per cent in the First World War) to 1991 (over 70 per cent in Operation Desert Storm).[18] Technology can bring in higher lethality in weapons and more efficiency in managing logistics, but it cannot eliminate or even reduce the need for physical transportation and the maintenance of men and material. As weapons became larger, complex and mobile, they required more fuel and a larger number of logistical troops to maintain and support them. For instance, the MI tank requires three times the fuel of earlier versions. In addition, there has been a trend of having more headquarters in modern armies. They are required for controlling non-combative support as well as combat elements. If the strength of the headquarters is clubbed with the tail, the teeth-to-tail ratio goes further down. The troop's welfare and morale has also taken a front seat in modern armies and hence, a lot has to be spent to give them the best. The reason for this primarily is that in the last 25 years, more and more lucrative jobs/opportunities have become available to people to earn a living, making it difficult for the armed

---

[18] Mcgrath, J. J. (2011). *The Other End of the Spear: The Tooth-to-Tail Ratio in Modern Military Operations.*

forces to attract the youth to join the uniformed fraternity.

The Siachen Glacier

The Siachen Glacier is a 70 km-long glacier that is occupied by the Pakistani and Indian troops around the year. At a height of 6,700 m, it is one of the highest battlefields in the world where temperatures can go down to -70°C. More people die due to climate than combat. Logistics and medical aid are extremely costly and difficult to provide. Only light helicopters can reach such heights and that too if the weather permits. The Indian Army estimates the cost at about $500,000 dollars a day to maintain a small force.

However, Siachen has political and psychological importance, else it does not make sense for both the armies to stay there. The Pakistanis cannot reach the top of the glacier due to its topology, while the Indians can't come down due to military reasons. Stephen P. Cohen of Brookings Institution, an expert on the Indian subcontinent, said 'This is like a struggle of two bald men over a comb.'[19] It is a battle over a barren land, which is costing both developing countries a fortune to maintain. With little teeth for that height, the tail is pretty huge and expensive.

The Air Force and the Navy

The air force is a very important part of a combat force. Within the armed forces, it is taken as a separate fighting entity. In the air force, evaluating the teeth-to-tail ratio may be simpler than the army, which has a very complex system. The air force has aircraft of all types that take part in combat and a few that are

---

[19] Raghavan, V. R. (2002). *Siachen: Conflict without end*. Viking Adult.

used for transporting cargo, troops or materials. In a way, all the aircraft including combat helicopters would constitute the teeth. The rest of the equipment and manpower at airports, like the air traffic control, maintenance, supplies and accounts, would constitute the tail. The lethal part of the force consists of aircraft like fighters, fighter-bombers, bombers, gunships, cargo, air force command and control aircraft, surveillance aircraft and helicopters.

The navy has its own importance in warfare. A country decides to invest in its naval power depending on the length of the coastline of a nation and its political objectives to dominate the sea. All ships with fighting capabilities form the teeth. Frigates, destroyers, corvettes, aircraft carriers and submarines deliver the punch. Others in the flotilla, like mine sweepers and patrol vessels, also play a pivotal role in war. A number of naval establishments other than the ships are required to be established on land, mostly near the coastline, to support the fighting element. These form the tail.

Lessons Learnt from These Military Operations

There are some very important lessons that can be learnt from the above. These are not only lessons for the military and the political class, but are equally important for any operation, campaign or project in a civilian setup. With shrinking turnaround time, the corporate world needs to be more agile and proactive to market requirements and the constantly changing business scenario.

High Priority

Logistical support must be given high priority. In a battlefield, the GS must not accord priority to operational tasks alone. It must realize the importance of logistics, which needs to fetch up at the speed of military operations. History is testimony that whenever commanders didn't accord enough priority to, and allocate resources for, logistics, they failed miserably. Battles and even wars have been lost due to this one single reason.

Detailed Planning

A principle established centuries ago, planning is the key to success. End-to-end planning, with written detailed instructions if possible, is very important for smooth and flawless logistical support, and should be passed onto all concerned. If the project execution is in a far-off location, then planning in advance becomes all the more critical.

Foresight

The military commander or the manager in charge needs to have the ability to visualize what is coming. In a military operation, the information available to the planning staff is often unreliable, and at times, incomplete. One has to learn to see through the fog. A similar situation exists while executing large-scale business projects.

The Build-up Must Be Done Before You Go Live

The necessary hardware and manpower must reach the desired location well in time. Moving in haste can be devastating. The head of operations must, therefore, give as much advance notice to the head of logistics as time permits.

Make Logistical Support an Integral Part of the Main Operational Planning

Once a military commander or a manager in charge of

operations allocates priority to logistical support, he must involve the in-charge of logistics in operational planning from the very beginning. This will ensure that logistical support remains in sync with the entire operational rollout.

Flexibility Is a Key Component

In any civil or military operation, there are unavoidable uncertainties and ambiguities. The logistical support planning staff must, therefore, keep this in mind and have an ace up their sleeves at all times to quickly react to a situation. Reserve resources must be kept centrally, which can be released to cater to any contingency.

Single-Window Clearance

As in Operation Desert Storm and also during Alexander's time, a single point of contact for all administrative requirements can be very useful. The only precaution one must take is to ensure enough decentralization is built into this, so that that single point does not become inaccessible or act like a bottleneck. Centralization will always hamper the operations.

Set Realistic Expectations

Go by the old saying 'Don't bite off more than what you can chew.' The Americans got into the Vietnamese conflict without realizing what was in store for them. For this assessment and appreciation, overall commitment is very necessary.

Don't Take on Operations Based on Emotions or Ego

While practical decisions may be necessary for a nation state due to political compulsions, which again may be influenced by public opinion, such opinion is dependent on the emotional response of the masses. This should certainly be avoided. The Siachen Glacier is a case in point. Both India and Pakistan have taken a stand and have created a messy situation for each other. For this, both the countries are paying a very heavy price. There has been a stalemate for the last thirty years because of the political and military ego of the two adversaries. 'Ego is the invisible line item on every company's profit and loss statement,' says David Marcum and Steven Smith in their book *Egonomics*.[20] Dr Paul Nutt of Ohio University, during his research, found out that almost 50 per cent of business decisions fail because decision-makers do not explore alternatives once they have made up their minds.[21] Secondly, most of these failed decisions (at least one-third of them) do not work out because they are driven by ego. You are likely to go wrong when you base your decision on what you like and not what will work. Take the following example for instance: Based on low-orbit satellites, Project Iridium was concieved by Barry Bertie, a Motorola engineer, when his wife was unable to make a cell phone call during a trip to the Bahamas. The company spent $7 billion and took 10 years to put this together, only to find that it was outdated when it was finally ready. The project was sold for $35 million to his top brass, basis his ego, and in turn, turned on the ego burners of his bosses to land them into deep financial trouble. This is not an example related to logistics, but is enough to demonstrate that decisions based on ego can be devastating.

In a broader context, the teeth-to-tail ratio may not remain

---

[20] Marcum, D., Smith, S., & Smith, S. B. (2008). *Egonomics: What makes ego our greatest asset (or most expensive liability)*. Simon and Schuster.
[21] Nutt, P. C. (2003). *Why decisions fail: Avoiding the blunders and traps that lead to debacles.*

a static figure for an army or an organization. For instance, the ratio would be quite different for a land war being fought in the plains as compared to a mountainous terrain.

Your Core Competence Is the Teeth

Looking at it another way, one needs to clearly understand one's actual line of business and focus on core competencies. The other functions become support functions and are subservient to the core area.

Telecom

A telco or cellular service provider (CSP) has to look at two major aspects while rolling out a telecom network. First is the network installation and equipment, which is the hardware required for a network. Second is the marketing part, which involves acquiring a customer base and providing customer service. Especially in India, most companies have outsourced their network installation and maintenance to equipment manufacturers. They, in turn, have identified marketing and customer care as their core area, which they treat as their key operations and support. Marketing feedback will also dictate adding or subtracting telecom hardware and the locations where expansion will take place.

For a CSP working in this way, marketing and customer care becomes the teeth and network installation and maintenance becomes the tail. Both the components are indispensable.

Education

An educational institute has two basic components. Firstly, the infrastructure (the hardware) and secondly, the quality of the faculty and teaching methodology (the software). In this case, though the hardware is important, excellence can be built only through good quality teaching. Here, the teeth is the software and the tail, the hardware.

Technology-driven Business

For product/software development and maintenance companies, their technology soldiers become the frontliners and are the teeth. The rest of the workforce becomes the tail. While you need to hire world-class technology people, you cannot neglect the HR, finance and facility management that'll provide the support.

The Concept of Ultimate Capacity

While planning a project, ultimate capacity is something that one must always keep in mind. In corporate jargon, one often finds that the concept of scalability is closely related to ultimate capacity. Those are applicable to almost every situation in one form or the other.

Military Operations

While planning, military commanders always keep unforeseen situations in mind. You plan to launch an operation with, say, 10,000 men and plan your forward airports and ammunition dumps only for this much. What if you need to induct 10,000 more?

Therefore, you need to use foresight to keep everything ready in advance for this additional requirement and peg a figure in your mind that could be the 'ultimate capacity' that you may need at some point of time.

Telecom Networks and Switches

While planning telecom networks, scalability is very important. Who could have imagined the rapid proliferation of mobile communications in developing economies 10 years ago. Planners must make room for additional spectrum availability and requirement. The installation of additional switches and equipment in the future should be considered. For static switches, or even to instal an electronic private branch exchange in the office premises, one must plan to have enough additional slots initially in the switch, so that as and when more lines are required, the capacity can be gradually enhanced by inserting additional cards. While one plans a communication network, all the requirements cannot be visualized; therefore, it is necessary to build additional capacity right at the beginning. Otherwise, when additional capacity is required, changing the complete hardware will be very expensive.

Roads and Transportation

Today, most cities are struggling to manage their road space against the onslaught of the ever-increasing number of cars and two-wheelers. The roads were planned according to what the planners could visualize say 50 years ago. Nobody could imagine that many people would have multiple cars, especially in developing countries. In future, road networks should be planned in a better way as regards to the ultimate capacity.

Town Planning

The concept of ultimate capacity must also apply to town planning. When new townships are planned, they must cater for population increase and rural-to-urban migration.

Similarly, this needs to be kept in mind while planning for airports too.

Industrial Organizations

While setting up new industries or offices, one must keep the scalability factor in mind and cater to future expansion.

Production vs Marketing

It is not easy to decipher what the teeth and the tail constitute, though one can make out a pattern. Business theory has undergone several changes in the last few decades, especially after the globalization of trade and economy have become a reality. One clear trend that has emerged is that marketing has certainly become very important for every business. The best of the products can fail if proper marketing is not done. In a competitive market, you cannot expect to create a good product and then sit back and wait for the orders to pour in on their own. Therefore, there is a challenge in selling products.

Companies invest substantially in R&D to bring out the best. But they cannot cut corners while marketing their products. There is no business today where marketing can be taken lightly. In fact, every business must view their product/offering from this view point and strike a balance between R&D, production cost and marketing efforts, though the methods and proportions may differ from industry to industry. Let us look at two examples where product is considered to be the king.

Books and Publishing

A book that has to sell at a particular price has to go through several hands before it reaches the customer. For instance, in a typical scenario, the book publisher distributes his product through distributers, who may have sub-distributors who then supply to the bookshops. A distributor keeps a margin for himself and so does the sub-distributor. Shopkeepers also need to make profits and hence, a book that has a print price of ₹100 fetches the publisher only ₹40–50 per copy. The publisher also has to pay royalty to the author and cover his production cost. He has to incur expenses on branding and advertising as well. Therefore, more than 60 per cent of the cost goes towards the marketing and distribution of the product. Here, creating the intellectual property is the teeth and marketing it is the tail. Clearly, the tail is larger than the teeth.

Movies

Today, the entertainment industry is all about marketing and promotion. With so many new movies hitting the market every week, a great movie that is badly marketed may just go unnoticed! On the other hand, an average movie, which is properly marketed and screened on several scenes simultaneously, will at least recover its cost in the first week of its release.

Technology as Teeth in Business

In case of warfare, technology plays a very big role in determining how wars are fought today. Similarly, in the last two decades, technology has changed the way marketing and distribution is done. Let us revisit the sales and marketing techniques of the above two industries, as well as a few others.

Books and Other Intellectual Content

Online shopping has changed the way books are distributed today. The conventional way of selling/buying books at bookshops is being rapidly replaced by readers ordering their copies online and often getting hefty discounts. Online portals don't have to maintain any inventory and only have to create a responsive supply chain backbone. This supply chain system will enable the portals to pick up the orders in almost real time from major distributors or publishers and deliver it at the doorsteps of the customer in a reasonable time frame. The customer does not have to go hunting around for a title from shop to shop and gets a free home delivery of almost any book under the sun that he desires to buy. Technology has become the marketing facilitator and is the cutting edge in the marketing space. Since the entire business model depends on marketing, it is very much a contender for being the teeth in the game. E-books have further made printing of books irrelevant, and maybe in a few decades, paperbacks may disappear altogether.

Movie Distribution

Digital cinema and high-quality satellite links have been a game changer for movie distribution. Film producers and distributers don't have to make those cumbersome heavy cans of celluloid films and transport them to different locations across the world. This is a flexible, efficient, versatile and cost-effective solution to cinema hall owners as well as film distributors. Moreover, proper promotion can result in enough heads showing up to watch the film and thus, redeeming the cost of the film very quickly.

Just-in-Time Inventory (JIT)

Using technology and other management techniques, JIT reduces the expenses of a company by keeping its inventory to the minimum possible extent. It ensures that the right quantity of the right material is available at the right place at the right time.

Education via Satellites

Technology has created virtual classrooms and now world-class lectures can be recorded and delivered to almost any part of the world, at a very low cost.

Innovative Thinking to Cut Costs of Production and Maintenance

The philosophy both in business and war should be to get maximum bang for the buck. Military thinkers and planners, therefore, keep coming up with new ideas to cut the cost of warfare. Similarly, business leaders come up with new methods to cut costs. Margins being thin today, cost reduction becomes a survival mantra. Whether by reducing the teeth or cutting the tail, costs must remain as low as possible.

The Israeli army realized that military-hardened equipment costs almost eight times the hardware available commercially. For example, a commercially available computer that has to meet military specifications has to have hardening from component upwards. All the semiconductor devices need to comply with stringent specifications, besides all the other components. Therefore, the cost becomes prohibitively high. A commercially available computer with the same configuration can also deliver a similar performance, but it may not withstand the extreme heat, dust, cold and bumps of a battlefield. It may become unserviceable earlier than a military-hardened machine. So what did they do? They replaced it with another similar commercial machine and got going. If there is a direct hit by a shell, whether hardened or not, both computers will get blown up. Therefore, for non-critical missions, they used commercial equipment, saving a great deal and without affecting the efficiency or compromising operational requirements.

US Defense Secretary Robert Gates proposed something similar. He intended to go for a greater number of systems that represent 75 per cent solution instead of smaller quantities of 99 per cent (exquisite systems). As long as it serves the purpose and saves the cost, it is well worth it.

11

Principle of 'One Leg on the Ground': Safety First

> 'Battles are won by slaughter and maneouver. The greater the general, the more he contributes in maneouver, the less he demands in slaughter.'
> —Winston Churchill

Introduction

The conduct of war is regulated by certain well-established and recognized rules, known as 'Laws of War'. They comprise of the rules, written or unwritten, for conducting war on land and sea. One of the potent Laws of War is 'safety first', or popularly known as 'one leg on the ground'. During military operations, this principle is not only applied by a soldier at an individual level, but is also kept in mind by military commanders while planning complex military operations, especially when formations need to work in tandem. The primary aim of the commanders should be to minimize the vulnerability of strategic plans, activities, relationships and systems to manipulation and interference by the enemy.

The key skill of an army commander in the battlefield is visualization. He should be able to have a bird-eye's view of the battlefield and have a feel for positioning. Manoeuvre in the battlefield is devised post visualization, and comprises land manoeuvre and air manoeuvre. The aim of manoeuvre is to gain position advantage relative to an adversary and can be utilized at all levels of warfare. These laws are taught as part of field craft to every soldier to move stealthily and effectively during battle, and can save a soldier's life during tactical moves like patrolling alongside or behind enemy lines, laying an ambush, or even during routine administrative moves that are conducted close to the enemy lines. When one walks at night in a jungle or a mountainous terrain, for instance, one can trip over natural obstacles like potholes, logs, boulders or thick undergrowth. One may also encounter ditches and artificial obstacles laid by the enemy. There can be booby traps, trip wires and low wire entanglements to impede movement. These can be avoided by using certain established drills.

Some stealth movements followed by soldiers are mentioned below:

The Ghost Walk

In the ghost walk or monkey run, a person lifts up one leg and gently puts the toe to feel for a safe spot to place the entire foot. One foot must be fully secured before the other one is moved off the ground. The soldier must use their empty hand to look for any wires or obstructions ahead of them. The soldier should not bend over because that position is tiring and limits restriction. The head should be positioned for clear observation. The idea is to develop a basic instinct about placing one foot on the ground firmly before lifting the other.

This principle is applicable to most field craft movements taught to a soldier. It is a standard drill for moving at night when visibility is very low, and can be a life saver.

Kitten Crawl

The kitten crawl is performed by crawling on the hands and knees. One should scrutinize the ground ahead for twigs with the right hand and carry their weapon in the left hand. When the area is clear of noise-making debris, the knees should be moved up to the right hand, and the method is then repeated.

Stomach Crawl

The stomach crawl is a quiet means of closing in on the enemy. One should lie on the stomach, search the ground ahead for twigs, dry leaves and trip wires with the right hand. The soldier should then lift the body with his forearms and toes, press it forward and lower it to the ground. The weapon should be in the left hand.

The platoon uses several mounted and dismounted formations and movement techniques to manoeuver in the battlefield. The wedge, column and line are specific forms of mounted formation. Dismounted formations include the squad formation and platoon formation. During a planned attack on the enemy following the fire and move tactics, two groups move one by one. One group gets firmly entrenched, ready to provide covering fire and only then does the other group move forward. Even in case of larger formations like battalions and brigades on the move, this principle is never violated. One formation first secures the ground, gets ready in all respects and only then is the other formation signalled to move. As children, we all watched Tarzan swing through jungles using tree vines as ropes. He first got a grip on a vine before he left the one he was hanging on to. Spiderman moved across buildings pretty much in the same way.

In the technology space, especially in electrical systems, a switch or relay is configured to make a first (i.e. connect) set of contacts before breaking (disconnecting) the old contacts. This prevents even a momentary disconnection of all the contacts simultaneously. Therefore, there is 'make before a break'. In the modern mobile CDMA cellular technology, the technique is more refined and is referred to as 'soft handoff'. Communication is provided in an area by systematically deploying several base transmitter stations (BTSs) to cover the entire area as a grid. Each BTS covers a small area called a cell, hence the name 'cellular'. A mobile subscriber moves in that grid crisscrossing through these cells, each providing a signal to the phone as long as it is in that cell. The CDMA signaling technology allows a cell phone to be connected to two or more BTSs simultaneously. When the mobile phone moves out of the area covered by one cell (BTS) to the area covered by another cell, the call is transferred to the second cell. Before the phone disconnects the old channel, it first latches on to the new channel covered by the new cell. With such wide applicability, this principle can be universally applied to our lives as well.

When parents or teachers tell their children to move cautiously, they often advise taking one step at a time. In an age where speed matters the most, such advice is many times not adhered to and one tends to throw caution to the wind, thereby paying a heavy price in the end.

This is a very important principle for those who want to become entrepreneurs as well. Today, the trend is not to work for someone, but go in for a venture of your own. Therefore, people are prepared to leave well-paying jobs to become their own masters. One can draw important lessons from the lives of successful entrepreneurs. The most difficult and trying time for an entrepreneur is when he switches over from a secure job to start a venture of his own. Many people make this switch when they are already married. Some even have children and a family to support. This transition, therefore, not only affects them, but impacts their families as well.

A new venture takes a while to establish and become profitable. The interim period is what one needs to cater for. One can have a smooth transition if one follows the principle of 'one leg on the ground'. This can be done by making adequate room for survival during the establishment phase. You don't have to dry out all your resources at once. For instance, one of the family members keeps his/her job, so that there is enough to put food on the table. Life can go on smoothly until the new venture is established. This is equally applicable to business expansion and diversification. Many establishments try to expand rapidly. Even if they have adequate resources, they are unable to control their quality as well as their operations at the desired pace and scale. It is better to consolidate first and then move cautiously, planning each action in advance.

12

Camouflage and Concealment: Merge with the background

> *'All warfare is based on deception. Hence, when able to attack, we must seem unable; when using our forces, we must seem inactive; when we are near, we must make the enemy believe we are far away; when far away, we must make him believe we are near.'*
>
> —Sun Tzu

Basic Military Requirement

The survival tactics of animals have inspired many inventions and ideas. 'Crypsis' is an ecological term defined as the ability of an organism to avoid detection by other organisms. Over a period of time, several animals, like lizards, snakes, birds, animals and fish, have evolved in such a way that they can/do resemble their surroundings. This helps them avoid detection by larger species that are out to prey on them. These animals could look like stones, sand or even plants. Methods used include nocturnality, camouflage or even mimicry.

Man has always learnt from nature. During a battle, it is important to protect men and material, and military personnel quickly learnt the trick of camouflage from animals and developed methods to achieve concealment.

Camouflage is the use of material and techniques or a combination of both, to make an object or an individual difficult to detect, and is applied to hide, disguise, decoy, blend or disrupt the impression of military targets and their backdrops. This prevents an enemy from locating friendly troops, arms, installations or activities. In the larger sense, this also means deceiving the enemy of your intentions. Therefore, you camouflage physically to camouflage your intentions.

Military camouflage and concealment developed very rapidly in the armed forces during the First World War. As the range, accuracy and lethality of firearms improved, the need to conceal men and material became such an important aspect of military operations that a lot of effort and thinking went into making it better and better. French artist Charles André Mare, who also served as a soldier in the French army during the First World War, developed military camouflage using special designs and techniques to deceive the human eye. Gradually, military camouflage formed a part of the overall military deception strategy, involving disguise, dummies and even mimicry. During the Second World War, dummy aircraft, dummy paratroopers and dummy tanks were deployed both by Allied as well as Axis forces. Since the war was fought across different terrains, a variety of camouflage techniques were developed. Troops fighting in jungles used different shades of green on their equipment and battle uniforms. In snow-bound areas, the clothing was snow white in colour. During desert warfare, the colour for the combat dress as well as vehicles and equipment was either khaki or a disruptive pattern using a mix of khaki and brown. Aircraft were also painted to avoid detection. Ships were painted in dazzle patterns to confuse the enemy regarding their speed and direction. Substantial research and effort went into making disruptive outlines and generating digital pixilated patterns.

The Role of Technology

As technology advanced, radars emerged on the scene. It was, thereafter, almost impossible for an aircraft to hide. Pilots had to resort to flying low to avoid being detected by enemy radars. To counter this, stealth technology was invented. This is also known as low-observation technology. In general, it is supposed to make ships, aircraft, submarines and missiles almost invisible to radars, sonar and infrared technology. It uses a combination of radar-absorbing material, non-metallic frames, disruptive non-reflective contours and shapes of the target to make the radar cross-section so small that it becomes very difficult for any radar system to detect the object.

Remaining underwater is the best way to remain unidentified. Therefore submarines were developed. They are usually painted black to avoid being detected, can remain as deep as 800 ft and move at 25 miles per hour, which is equivalent of 45 km per hour. Many carry submarine-launched ballistic missiles and therefore, have tremendous destructive power. They were well used during the Second World War, and during the Cold War period, both Americans and the Soviets invested heavily in submarine technology. Nuclear-powered submarines can remain submerged for a very long period. Food and supplies are the only limitation on the submergence time and thus, a 90-day supply is usually carried on board.

Spies and Moles

To gather intelligence, spies operate in the enemy territory and moles are planted in enemy organizations. Such people have to hide their identity and operate for years to pass relevant information back home. Undercover operators have to acquire a complete new identity and become part of the new country or organization. To be able to operate without being detected, they also have to learn the language, mannerisms and culture of the country they operate in.

Role in the Civilian Environment

Concealment, camouflage and blending in with the background are equally important while doing business, especially in a global environment. For individuals seeking a global role or working with a diverse, ethnic workforce, blending and merging with the crowd is the key to success.

The principles of camouflage and concealment can also be used very effectively at a personal level, and has to be cleverly adapted by every individual so as to mesh and merge with the environment. 'In Rome, do as the Romans do' is an old adage that comes to one's mind when looking at this concept. In its simplest form, it means the ability to merge with the changed environment. You observe the customs, dressing habits and mannerisms of the new organization and quickly, yet intelligently, mould yourself to become 'one of them'.

Cultural fit becomes a big challenge for those who underestimate its importance. When civil servants as well as the armed forces personnel get into the corporate world after retirement, they face a very different environment. Those who observe, adapt and are willing to accept the change do very well in their new innings. However, those who resist the change find it difficult to sustain themselves. Similarly, people working in the corporate sector face a cultural shock while moving into the public sector. It would be prudent to quickly learn the ropes of the trade and merge with the new environment.

Cross-culture management is becoming extremely

important in today's globalized world. Organizations are making a very conscious effort to manage cross-cultural diversity. There are differences among employees and if these differences are managed properly, employees can turn into great assets and bring in more productivity and efficiency. Diversity, in terms of gender, age, work experience, knowledge, culture, race and even religion, has to be kept in mind. One of the key principles of diversity management is that every individual has to contribute positively to the group or the organization. When an individual starts accepting these differences amongst coworkers and learns to be in harmony, in a way he tries to 'merge with' the multicultural work environment that has emerged out of such a heterogeneous group.

In operational terms and the day-to-day dealings with people and situations, it is important to understand what others expect from you. It is also important to understand and appreciate what their traditions, values and customs are. For example, if you are dealing with Arabs, it is for you to realize that their sense of punctuality is quite different from that of Western nations. Their decisions are based more on emotions rather than logic. During meetings, there may be interruptions, which, for many people, are strange. In the Arab world, local connections are very important for running a business or cracking a deal. There is a good amount of bureaucratic red tape and one must cater for such delays in the entire business plan.

If one compares Chinese and Americans, then Americans are willing to discuss their very personal problems like a divorce with their colleagues at work. Chinese and other Asians will keep these things very close to their chest and share it only with those who are like family. Similarly, Americans commonly use foul language, but Filipinos won't take it kindly if you say, 'Don't be stupid!' to your colleague.

While marketing products and concepts globally, one has to adapt products to local tastes and conditions. In India, pizzas and burgers need to have a few vegetarian variants. Cars also need to have higher ground clearances as the road conditions are not very good in a majority of the areas.

Another form of camouflage that is frequently employed now is surrogate advertising. This technique is used to promote certain harmful products like liquor, cigarettes or chewing tobacco in disguise. For instance, a company could use music CDs or even water to promote liquor. Usually, a product close to the category is chosen for this purpose. For example, club soda, fruit juices or playing cards with the same brand name could be used to promote alcoholic drinks.

Camouflage, concealment and merging with the background must be used by organizations to manage diversity in their branding and advertising campaigns. This must also be kept in mind while designing their products meant for different markets. It is an equally important concept for individuals when they work with people of different origins.

13

Selection and Maintenance of Aim: Vision and Mission

> *'Pursue one great decisive aim with force and determination.'*
>
> —Carl Von Clausewitz

Out of the 10 principles of war, selection and maintenance of aim are considered as the master principles of military strategy. A single unambiguous aim is the cornerstone of a successful military operation. War is a means to achieve a political objective and therefore, this objective has to be taken into account while formulating a military strategy, which tends to be long drawn in its evolution, execution and after-effects. The perfect selection of an overarching goal or aim is the crucial keystone for a successful military strategy.

The earliest known principles of war were laid down and documented by Sun Tzu in 500 BCE. Later, military generals and thinkers created different versions as they gained experience while participating in several campaigns. General Carl Von Clausewitz, a Prussian general and military theorist, devoted considerable time and effort to develop a philosophy of war. He used campaigns of Fredrick the Great and Napoleon as frames of reference to draw his own inferences. His work is still studied and quoted in military discussions. His famous commonly use foul language, but Filipinos won't take it kindly if you say, 'Don't be stupid!' to your colleague.

While marketing products and concepts globally, one has to adapt products to local tastes and conditions. In India, pizzas and burgers need to have a few vegetarian variants. Cars also need to have higher ground clearances as the road conditions are not very good in a majority of the areas.

Another form of camouflage that is frequently employed now is surrogate advertising. This technique is used to promote certain harmful products like liquor, cigarettes or chewing tobacco in disguise. For instance, a company could use music CDs or even water to promote liquor. Usually, a product close to the category is chosen for this purpose. For example, club soda, fruit juices or playing cards with the same brand name could be used to promote alcoholic drinks.

Camouflage, concealment and merging with the background must be used by organizations to manage diversity in their branding and advertising campaigns. This must also be kept in mind while designing their products meant for different markets. It is an equally important concept for individuals when they work with people of different origins.

13

Selection and Maintenance of Aim: Vision and Mission

> *'Pursue one great decisive aim with force and determination.'*
>
> —Carl Von Clausewitz

Out of the 10 principles of war, selection and maintenance of aim are considered as the master principles of military strategy. A single unambiguous aim is the cornerstone of a successful military operation. War is a means to achieve a political objective and therefore, this objective has to be taken into account while formulating a military strategy, which tends to be long drawn in its evolution, execution and after-effects. The perfect selection of an overarching goal or aim is the crucial keystone for a successful military strategy.

The earliest known principles of war were laid down and documented by Sun Tzu in 500 BCE. Later, military generals and thinkers created different versions as they gained experience while participating in several campaigns. General Carl Von Clausewitz, a Prussian general and military theorist, devoted considerable time and effort to develop a philosophy of war. He used campaigns of Fredrick the Great and Napoleon as frames of reference to draw his own inferences. His work is still studied and quoted in military discussions. His famous quote 'War is the continuation of politics by other means' neatly sums up the need to wage war and its ultimate aim.

Clausewitz, while developing his philosophy, further refined the principle of 'selection and maintenance of aim' by linking it to the end state, the ultimate political objective that needs to be achieved through military operations. Today, therefore, three services—the army, navy and air force—need to be in absolute synchronization with each other and supported by the political hierarchy as well as government departments. Considering the geopolitical conditions, military planners must also understand and consider the military conditions and alliances of the enemy within the regional and international arenas while formulating a realistic goal, which is defined unambiguously by the aim. Once the aim is decided, all efforts are directed to attain this goal. Every action and plan must be checked for its impact on the chosen aim. Therefore, each operation and every phase of war must be directed towards the fulfilment of the supreme aim. As the military campaign develops, the military operational aim may need to be reviewed and modified; this should be approved at the highest level.

Selection and maintenance of aim are equally important in the business environment. If it is the master principle of war, it can also be seen as a fundamental tenet for setting up a business and then ensuring its success in the end. In corporate parlance, the positioning of an organization with respect to its customers, environment and all other stakeholders is defined in terms of a vision and mission statement.

Vision is long-term, futuristic, broad-based and inspirational in its tenor. It also defines the desired end state, clearly stating where you want to reach. Mission is about today and gives the specifics about how to achieve the defined goals. It broadly defines the processes and operations involved. For instance, given below are the vision and mission statements of the Wockhardt Hospitals.

Vision

'Wockhardt Hospitals will strive with excellence to fulfil the needs of the community in its chosen field of medical treatment.'

Mission

'To serve and enrich the quality of life of patients suffering from diseases, through the efficient deployment of technology and human expertise, in a caring and nurturing environment with the greatest respect for human dignity and life.'

- Wockhardt Hospitals believe in setting the best practice standards in our services, continuously improving performance and exceeding the expectations of our patients as well as their families. We believe in building and maintaining long-term patient relationships, so as to become an essential resource for their well-being. We believe in:
- Training and developing the best human resource as the key to deliver superior patient service
- Consistently investing in technology and infrastructure to match international benchmarks
- Leading the development of professional standards in healthcare management
- Continuously educating the community about the prevention of cardiac disorders

Military aim states the result alone and all operations are planned to achieve this supreme aim. Simply put, the vision statement is like a military aim and the mission statement is akin to operational orders and military planning. The major difference between war and business is that war has to end after the aim has been achieved, but business must go on according to the vision that was set for its very raison d'être.

In the corporate setup, vision defines the future of the organization and hence, does not really change. The mission could change according to the business environment, akin to military tactics undergoing change due to battlefield imperatives. Ultimately, the idea is to always fetch up to the vision statement.

One thing that is common between the military aim and the corporate vision is that both should be clear and simple.

IBM

International Business Machines, now simply known as IBM, was one of the key players in the computer business. The company focused on manufacturing computer machines and for a long time, mainframe computers. With the advent of technology, when mini and microcomputers emerged on the scene, they quickly shifted their business focus to smaller computers and came up with personal computers, or PCs, with the launch of IBM-PC. They did successfully achieve their aim of market dominance in producing computer hardware.

Microsoft

Microsoft, on the other hand, focused on computer software and that too in the microcomputer range. Their flagship product being MS Office, they literally put fuel into almost every machine that was produced. Their belief was that there is money in the software, rather than manufacturing and selling the boxes. They did not falter as far as their aim was concerned, and moved on to Windows 95 and Windows 98, introducing the 'click and drag' function. This revolutionized the way people used computers. Remaining yet again in the software space, they came up with the MS Office suite.

Google

Right from the beginning, Google aimed at developing the best and the most optimized search engines. From the time the founders of Google started the company, their aim was very clear—to dominate Internet searches. And their mission was stated in a dozen simple words: 'To organize the world's information and make it universally accessible and useful.'

They first wanted to be an Internet giant in their own space, for which they provided their facility free of cost to their users. Later, they came up with a business model with advertising-based revenue. The founders described their product in simple words: 'Our perfect search engine would understand exactly what you mean and give back what you want. Google was successful precisely because we were better and faster and finding the right answers than other search engines at that time.'

They still concentrate on Internet search, as that was their core competence, though they created related search products based on the demand by users.

Apple

Apple focused on the hardware-software combo, and their aim can be judged through one of their official statements: 'Apple is committed to bringing the best computing experience to its users around the world through its innovative hardware, software and Internet offerings.'

The company's aim is clearly innovation in the space of computing. They thus designed and brought out high-end laptops called Macs, along with professional software like iLife and iWork. They also created iPods, iPads and iPhones, redefining the future of mobile computing devices.

The aim as visualized in their vision remained the same, but they changed their products, operations and technology as per the demands of time.

14

Tactical Retreat: How Far Is Too Far?

> *'To withdraw isn't a sign of weakness. It is a sign that a man knows the limits of his capabilities and the most probable outcome of the future. One who retreats to fight another day isn't running away, but looking for another road towards the same destination.'*
>
> —Lionel Suggs

Retreat, Reorganize and Hit Back

During a battle, it may happen that one side is attacked by an overwhelmingly large enemy force, resulting in a near defeat. In such a situation, troops abandon their location to avoid being killed or captured by the enemy. The commander in such a scenario has no control over his forces and defeat is imminent. This could happen due to cowardice, panic or even misinformation, resulting in chaos as well as loss of men and material. Of all the war operations, a withdrawal or retreat under acute enemy pressure is the most perilous and difficult.

On the other hand, there can be situations where the commander realizes that it would be prudent to move back a little in an organized way to avoid casualties and possibly consolidate forces to occupy ground in the rear, which is easily defendable. In such a scenario, a proper, organized retreat or withdrawal is undertaken under the orders of the unified command. Such a retreat is pre-planned, well-rehearsed and co-opted into the operation plan as a possible contingency plan.

A retreat or withdrawal is then undertaken as a military operation, which means moving back forces from the existing position in an orderly manner. If it is not undertaken as a deliberate and organized operation or if adequate control is not exercised, it can become a 'rout'. This implies a situation where troops move in a disorganized way, giving the enemy a greater chance of inflicting more and more damage. Therefore, a retreat is a risky operation that requires discipline, good communication and firm control.

Such an operation is termed as a 'tactical retreat,' which is based out of genuine tactical reasons and prevailing circumstances, rather than a knee jerk reaction to a heavy onslaught by the enemy forces. Here, the idea is to take tactical advantage by moving into a rear location, even at the cost of losing some territory. Such an act could also be planned to bring the enemy or lure him into an area where an ambush can be launched. Such an ambush could cause heavy causalities and losses, and may even turn the tide.

The ultimate aim is to retreat, consolidate, reorganize and hit back to finally defeat the enemy. To achieve this on several occasions, 'a feigned rout' is planned, where your troops pretend that they have lost their nerve and are running disarrayed. This deception is planned to fool the enemy and gradually lure him into an area to launch a prepared ambush, thereby inflicting heavy casualties on the enemy.

A military mind regards retreat as dishonourable and disgraceful. Therefore, it is not easy for a commander to think of retreat, even if the tactical situation so demands. But it is a wise decision to go for it if you can save lives, avoid bloodshed, regain your strength and launch an offence at a later point of time when you are ready for it. This is an act of prudence, requiring foresight, judgement, maturity and even circumspection on the part of the military commander.

An organized retreat, if executed properly, can also be viewed as a victory. First, it can damage the morale of the enemy. The overenthusiastic, charged-up enemy troops get demoralized as they find their target disappearing in front of them. They often get confused and could even lose their killing instinct for a while. Second, the enemy commanders feel cheated, as the opportunity of a seemingly easy victory is lost. They are forced to change some of their plans at the tactical as well as strategic levels. A large, available force is rendered useless and it cannot be redeployed easily, as they do not have any ready plans for such an eventuality. This is common in guerilla warfare as well.

While withdrawing, it is prudent not to leave any equipment, ammunition or resources that can be of use to the enemy. The retreating forces should either carry all that is available back with them, or adopt the scorched earth policy. Joseph Stalin used this very effectively against the German army during the Second World War, and William Tecumseh Sherman during the American Civil War.

Retreating in Business and Personal Life

Tactical retreat is a concept that is quite relevant to businesses as well as our daily lives. Whether or not to opt for a tactical retreat is a matter of judgement and forethought. In a business environment, unlike a battlefield, there is a little more time available for consultations and discussions and probably, lesser stress.

For example, if a company has launched a new product after investing in R&D and discovers that their market research team had overestimated the market size, it only has two options: either to keep pumping more money into promotional efforts and thus, keep losing the money; or take a conscious decision to discontinue the product for a much smaller loss. It may have the same psychological impact for the company's leadership as it would for a battlefield commander ordering a tactical retreat, but the net result is beneficial in both cases.

At a personal level also, it is extremely important to understand 'how far is too far'. This is one of the major aspects of emotional intelligence. If armed goons are mugging you in a dark alley, there is no point putting up a fight and being killed or badly injured. It would be better to give them whatever you have to save your life and probably later go and lodge a police complaint. Politics is no different and tactical retreat is sometimes essential. Political compulsions, unforeseen circumstances and ground realities of the day force political parties to undertake tactical withdrawals. Delay tactics are also used commonly when coalition governments have to function. In many cases, such retreats become the survival mantra.

Tactical retreat is not only applicable to situations in modern warfare, but has been very effectively developed and used in Shaolin Kung Fu and other forms of unarmed combat. In essence, it involves moving back very swiftly when the opponent attacks, remaining in that position for a while and then going for a swift counter-attack. This is coupled with another Kung Fu principle: 'Striking the opponent when his old strength has been spent, but his new strength has not been created.' Similarly, in military warfare, tactical retreat sometimes makes the enemy very bold and overconfident and could lead his tired forces into a trap.

> *'So in war, the way is to avoid what is strong, and strike at what is weak.'*
>
> —Sun Tzu

Bibliography

Tefler, T. (2014, April 9). 'Dr. Zhivago' Used as Anti-Soviet Cold War Propaganda, According to Declassified CIA Documents. Retrieved from https://www.bustle.com/articles/20441-dr-zhivago-used-as-anti-soviet-cold-war-propaganda-according-to-declassified-cia-documents

Bedin, D. (2018). Theater of Operations. Retrieved from http://www.history-online.com/dday/en/strategy/theater/#deception

Winterbotham, F. W. (1999). *The Ultra Secret*. Weidenfeld and Nicolson.

Security and Secrecy. (2014, June 5). Retrieved from https://www.atomicheritage.org/history/security-and-secrecy

Johnson, R. (2010, April 25). Ten of the greatest battlefield tactics, by Rob Johnson. Retrieved from https://www.dailymail.co.uk/home/moslive/article-1267536/Ten-greatest-battlefield-tactics-Rob-Johnson.html

Perry, W. (1998, October 30). Information Technology as a Force Multiplier. Retrieved from https://www.hoover.org/research/information-technology-force-multiplier

Department of the Air Force. (June 1991). Air Force Stealth Technology Review. Retrieved from http://nsarchive.gwu.edu/NSAEBB/NSAEBB443/docs/area51_14.PDF

Simkin, J. (1997, September). Heinz Guderian. Retrieved from http://spartacus-educational.com/GERguderian.htm

Griffith, S. B. (1963). *Sun Tzu: The Art of War* (Vol. 39). London: Oxford University Press.

Dittman, M. (June 2003). Operation hearts and minds. Retrieved from http://www.apa.org/monitor/jun03/operation.aspx

Weapons of Terror. (July 2014). Retrieved from http://www.

geospatialworld.net/article/weapons-of-terror/

Klein, C. (2014). Fooling Hitler: The Elaborate Ruse Behind D-Day. Retrieved from https://www.history.com/news/fooling-hitler-the-elaborate-ruse-behind-d-day

PLUTO, Secret Pipelines of WW II. (2010). Retrieved from http://aoghs.org/petroleum-in-war/secret-pipelines/

Vietnam War. (n.d.). Retrieved from https://www.historynet.com/vietnam-war

Techniques of employing Camouflage, Cover and Concealment (CCD). (n.d.). Retrieved from https://www.armystudyguide.com/content/army_board_study_guide_topics/camo_and_concealment/techniques-of-employing-camouflage-cover-and-concealment.shtml

Garber, M. (2013). Ghost Army: The Inflatable Tanks That Fooled Hitler. Retrieved from https://www.theatlantic.com/technology/archive/2013/05/ghost-army-the-inflatable-tanks-that-fooled-hitler/276137/